I0844996

Mastering
QUALITY MANAGEMENT
Concepts, Techniques, and Applications

Nikhilesh Mishra,
Author

Website
https://www.nikhileshmishra.com

Copyright Information

Copyright © 2023 Nikhilesh Mishra

All rights reserved. No part of this publication may be reproduced, distributed, or transmitted in any form or by any means, including photocopying, recording, or other electronic or mechanical methods, without the prior written permission of the publisher, except in the case of brief quotations embodied in critical reviews and certain other noncommercial uses permitted by copyright law.

For permissions requests, write to the publisher at the address below:

Nikhilesh Mishra

Website: **https://www.nikhileshmishra.com**

Disclaimer: The information contained in this book is for educational and informational purposes only. It is not intended as a substitute for professional advice. The author and publisher disclaim any liability for the use of any information provided in this book.

Trademarks: All brand names and product names used in this book are trade names, service marks, trademarks, or registered trademarks of their respective owners.

Dedication

This book is lovingly dedicated to the cherished memory of my father, **Late Krishna Gopal Mishra**, and my mother**, Mrs. Vijay Kanti Mishra.** Their unwavering support, guidance, and love continue to inspire me.

Table of Contents

Author's Preface

Welcome to the captivating world of the knowledge we are about to explore! Within these pages, we invite you to embark on a journey that delves into the frontiers of information and understanding.

Charting the Path to Knowledge

Dive deep into the subjects we are about to explore as we unravel the intricate threads of innovation, creativity, and problem-solving. Whether you're a curious enthusiast, a seasoned professional, or an eager learner, this book serves as your gateway to gaining a deeper understanding.

Your Guiding Light

From the foundational principles of our chosen field to the advanced frontiers of its applications, we've meticulously crafted this book to be your trusted companion. Each chapter is an expedition, guided by expertise and filled with practical insights to empower you on your quest for knowledge.

What Awaits You

- **Illuminate the Origins:** Embark on a journey through the historical evolution of our chosen field, discovering key milestones that have paved the way for breakthroughs.

- **Demystify Complex Concepts:** Grasp the fundamental principles, navigate intricate concepts, and explore practical applications.

- **Mastery of the Craft:** Equip yourself with the skills and knowledge needed to excel in our chosen domain.

Your Journey Begins Here

As we embark on this enlightening journey together, remember that mastery is not just about knowledge but also the wisdom to apply it. Let each chapter be a stepping stone towards unlocking your potential, and let this book be your guide to becoming a true connoisseur of our chosen field.

So, turn the page, delve into the chapters, and immerse yourself in the world of knowledge. Let curiosity be your compass, and let the pursuit of understanding be your guide.

Begin your expedition now. Your quest for mastery awaits!

Sincerely,

Nikhilesh Mishra,

Author

CHAPTER 1

Introduction to Quality Management

Quality is a universal pursuit that transcends industries and sectors, defining the very essence of excellence. In a world where products and services have become increasingly complex and competitive, the need for effective Quality Management has never been more critical. This chapter serves as our gateway into the realm of Quality Management, where we embark on a journey to explore its definition, historical evolution, key concepts, principles, and the profound impact it holds on organizations and their quest for perfection. Welcome to a world where quality reigns supreme, and its mastery becomes the key to enduring success.

A. Definition and Significance of Quality

In the realm of quality management, understanding the fundamental concept of quality is the cornerstone upon which all other principles and practices are built. Quality, in its essence, is a multifaceted concept that encompasses various dimensions and holds distinct significance across industries and contexts.

The Definition of Quality:

Quality is often defined as the degree to which a product, service, or process meets or exceeds customer expectations and complies with predefined standards or specifications. This definition underscores the primary goal of quality management, which is to consistently deliver products and services that not only meet but ideally surpass the requirements and desires of the customer.

Quality can be further dissected into several key attributes, including:

1. **Performance:** The primary function or purpose of the product or service must be met efficiently and effectively. For instance, a high-quality automobile should perform reliably, providing smooth transportation.

2. **Reliability:** Quality products and services should function without errors or defects over a specified period. Customers should be able to depend on them consistently.

3. **Durability:** The lifespan of a product or the longevity of a service should be commensurate with customer expectations and the intended usage. Durability speaks to the product's ability to withstand wear and tear over time.

4. **Features:** Extra features or attributes can enhance a product's

quality. These features may go beyond basic functionality and cater to specific customer needs or preferences.

5. **Conformance:** Products and services should adhere to established standards, specifications, or regulatory requirements. Conformance ensures that the quality is consistent and can be objectively measured.

6. **Aesthetics:** In some cases, the visual appeal of a product or the ambiance of a service environment can significantly impact perceived quality.

The Significance of Quality:

Quality is of paramount significance for several reasons:

1. **Customer Satisfaction:** Quality directly influences customer satisfaction. Satisfied customers are more likely to become repeat customers, recommend the product or service to others, and contribute to the organization's positive reputation.

2. **Competitive Advantage:** In today's highly competitive business landscape, quality can be a key differentiator. Organizations that consistently deliver high-quality products or services often gain a competitive edge.

3. **Cost Savings:** High-quality products and services are less likely to experience defects, failures, or customer complaints. This leads to reduced rework, returns, warranty claims, and

associated costs.

4. **Market Reputation:** A track record of quality builds trust and credibility with customers and stakeholders. A positive reputation can be a valuable asset for an organization.

5. **Legal and Regulatory Compliance:** Many industries are subject to stringent quality standards and regulations. Compliance is not just a legal requirement but also a crucial aspect of ensuring the safety and well-being of customers.

6. **Continuous Improvement:** Quality management encourages a culture of continuous improvement. By regularly assessing and enhancing processes, organizations can achieve higher levels of efficiency and effectiveness.

7. **Employee Engagement:** Engaged and motivated employees play a vital role in maintaining and improving quality. When employees feel their work contributes to a quality outcome, job satisfaction and morale tend to be higher.

In conclusion, the definition and significance of quality extend far beyond mere product inspection or service delivery. Quality embodies a commitment to meeting customer needs and expectations while striving for excellence, continuous improvement, and organizational success. It serves as the compass that guides organizations on their path toward achieving and sustaining excellence in an ever-evolving world.

B. Historical Evolution of Quality Management

The historical evolution of quality management is a fascinating journey that spans centuries and reflects the evolving understanding of what constitutes quality and how to achieve it. This evolution has been marked by significant milestones, prominent figures, and transformative shifts in thinking. Understanding this history provides valuable insights into the foundations of modern quality management.

Early Origins:

1. **Craftsmanship Era (Pre-19th Century):** Quality, in the early days, was largely synonymous with craftsmanship. Skilled artisans and craftsmen took great pride in producing goods of exceptional quality. However, quality control was often an informal process, relying on the craftsmanship of individual artisans.

2. **Industrial Revolution (Late 18th to Early 19th Century):** The industrial revolution marked a pivotal point in the history of quality. Mass production brought about concerns of consistency and uniformity in products. Early efforts in quality management emerged with a focus on inspection and controlling defects during manufacturing.

Pioneers in Quality:

3. **Walter Shewhart (1920s):** Often regarded as the father of statistical quality control, Shewhart developed statistical process control (SPC) methods. His work laid the foundation for understanding and controlling process variation, a critical aspect of quality management.

4. **W. Edwards Deming (1940s-1950s):** Deming's influence on quality management cannot be overstated. He introduced the concept of Total Quality Management (TQM) and emphasized the importance of statistical methods, continuous improvement, and a focus on customer needs. Deming's work became instrumental in Japan's post-World War II economic recovery.

5. **Joseph M. Juran (1950s):** Juran is known for his contributions to quality management through the Juran Trilogy: quality planning, quality control, and quality improvement. His emphasis on management's role in quality and the importance of employee involvement became core principles in TQM.

The Era of Total Quality Management (TQM):

6. **1970s-1980s:** Total Quality Management gained widespread recognition as a comprehensive approach to quality. It emphasized customer focus, continuous improvement,

employee involvement, and process-driven quality control. TQM became a global movement, with organizations worldwide adopting its principles.

The Emergence of International Quality Standards:

7. **ISO 9000 Series (1987):** The International Organization for Standardization (ISO) introduced the ISO 9000 series, providing a standardized framework for quality management systems. ISO 9001 became a benchmark for quality assurance and certification.

Lean and Six Sigma:

8. **Lean Thinking (1980s):** Originating from Toyota's production system, lean thinking focuses on eliminating waste, improving efficiency, and maximizing value. It complements TQM principles and is widely used in manufacturing and service industries.

9. **Six Sigma (1986):** Developed by Motorola, Six Sigma is a data-driven methodology for reducing defects and variations in processes. It emphasizes the importance of achieving near-perfect quality by minimizing process variation.

Contemporary Trends:

10. **Quality 4.0 (21st Century):** Quality 4.0 integrates emerging technologies like data analytics, the Internet of Things (IoT),

and artificial intelligence into quality management. It aims to enhance predictive quality, real-time monitoring, and agility in response to changing customer needs.

11. **Sustainability and Environmental Quality (21st Century):** The focus on sustainability has led to the integration of environmental considerations into quality management. Organizations are increasingly recognizing the importance of eco-friendly practices and sustainable supply chains.

Conclusion:

The historical evolution of quality management reflects a continuous journey of refinement and adaptation. From craftsmanship to modern methodologies like Lean, Six Sigma, and Quality 4.0, the quest for quality has evolved to encompass not only product or service excellence but also customer satisfaction, process optimization, and sustainability. This rich history serves as a foundation for contemporary quality management practices, emphasizing the enduring importance of quality in a rapidly changing world.

C. Key Concepts (Quality Standards, Total Quality Management)

The key concepts of quality management, including quality standards and Total Quality Management (TQM), are foundational principles that guide organizations in their pursuit of excellence, customer satisfaction, and continuous improvement.

Quality Standards:

Quality standards are the bedrock of consistent and reliable quality. They provide a framework for defining, measuring, and ensuring quality in products, services, and processes. Some of the most prominent quality standards include:

1. **ISO 9000 Series:** The ISO 9000 family of standards, developed by the International Organization for Standardization (ISO), outlines the requirements for a Quality Management System (QMS). ISO 9001 is the most well-known standard and focuses on processes and customer satisfaction. Compliance with ISO 9001 is often a prerequisite for conducting business globally.

2. **ISO 14001:** This standard focuses on Environmental Management Systems (EMS) and helps organizations manage their environmental responsibilities. It is closely related to sustainability and responsible business practices.

3. **ISO 45001:** ISO 45001 is the standard for Occupational Health and Safety Management Systems (OH&S MS). It helps organizations ensure a safe and healthy workplace for employees and stakeholders.

4. **AS9100:** This standard is specific to the aerospace industry and ensures product safety and reliability in aviation, space, and defense.

5. **ISO/TS 16949:** Formerly known as ISO/TS 16949, IATF 16949 sets the quality management system requirements for the automotive industry, emphasizing defect prevention and reduction of variation and waste.

6. **Good Manufacturing Practices (GMP):** GMP regulations are critical in the pharmaceutical and food industries, ensuring product safety, quality, and consistency.

7. **CMMI (Capability Maturity Model Integration):** CMMI is a framework used in software and systems engineering to assess and improve processes. It helps organizations achieve higher levels of maturity in their processes, resulting in improved product quality.

Total Quality Management (TQM):

Total Quality Management is a comprehensive approach to quality that involves all aspects of an organization, from its culture to its processes. TQM emphasizes the following key principles:

1. **Customer Focus:** TQM starts with understanding and meeting customer needs and expectations. Organizations actively seek customer feedback and use it to drive

improvements.

2. **Continuous Improvement:** A cornerstone of TQM is the belief that processes can always be improved. The Plan-Do-Check-Act (PDCA) cycle is often used to guide continuous improvement efforts.

3. **Employee Involvement:** Employees are seen as valuable resources in TQM. Their knowledge, skills, and commitment to quality are harnessed through empowerment and involvement in decision-making.

4. **Process-Centric Approach:** TQM encourages a process-centric view of an organization. Processes are analyzed, optimized, and controlled to achieve consistent quality outcomes.

5. **Data-Driven Decision Making:** TQM relies on data and measurement to make informed decisions. Statistical tools and analysis are used to monitor and improve processes.

6. **Supplier Relationships:** TQM recognizes the importance of supplier quality. Organizations work closely with suppliers to ensure the quality of incoming materials and components.

7. **Leadership and Commitment:** TQM requires strong leadership committed to quality. Leaders set the vision, create a culture of quality, and provide the necessary resources for

quality improvement.

8. **Strategic Alignment:** TQM aligns quality objectives with the organization's strategic goals. Quality becomes an integral part of the business strategy.

9. **Prevention over Inspection:** TQM emphasizes preventing defects and problems rather than relying solely on inspection and correction after the fact.

Conclusion:

Quality standards and Total Quality Management are two fundamental concepts that shape the quality landscape in organizations. Quality standards provide a structured approach to ensuring product or service quality, while TQM represents a holistic philosophy and methodology for achieving excellence. Together, these concepts lay the foundation for organizations to deliver superior quality, drive customer satisfaction, and continuously improve their processes and products.

D. Quality Management Principles

Quality management principles are the guiding tenets that underpin the philosophy and practices of effective quality management. Developed by various organizations and experts in the field, these principles provide a framework for achieving consistent and high-quality outcomes. Understanding and implementing these principles is essential for organizations aiming to excel in quality management.

The Core Quality Management Principles:

1. **Customer Focus:** The paramount principle of quality management is a relentless focus on customers. Organizations must understand and meet customer needs, expectations, and preferences. This principle underscores the importance of delivering products and services that not only meet but ideally exceed customer requirements.

2. **Leadership:** Quality begins at the top. Effective leadership is essential in setting a clear quality vision, creating a culture of quality, and providing the resources and support necessary for quality initiatives to succeed. Leaders should lead by example and actively champion quality.

3. **Engagement of People:** Recognizing that people are the heart of any organization, this principle emphasizes the importance of engaging and empowering employees at all levels. Engaged employees are more likely to contribute their skills, creativity, and commitment to achieving and maintaining high quality.

4. **Process Approach:** Quality management encourages organizations to view their activities as interconnected processes. By understanding, optimizing, and managing these

processes, organizations can ensure consistent and predictable quality outcomes. The Plan-Do-Check-Act (PDCA) cycle is often used to guide process improvement.

5. **Systematic Approach to Management:** Quality management is not a piecemeal effort but a systematic one. Organizations should adopt a structured and integrated approach to managing quality. This includes having a documented Quality Management System (QMS) that defines roles, responsibilities, and processes.

6. **Continual Improvement:** The pursuit of excellence is an ongoing journey. Organizations should continually seek opportunities to improve their processes, products, and services. The principles of continuous improvement, often associated with Total Quality Management (TQM), guide this effort.

7. **Factual Approach to Decision Making:** Informed decisions are critical to quality management. Organizations should base their decisions on data, evidence, and analysis rather than assumptions or intuition. This principle emphasizes the importance of data-driven decision-making.

8. **Mutually Beneficial Supplier Relationships:** Suppliers are essential partners in the supply chain. Organizations should establish and nurture mutually beneficial relationships with suppliers, collaborating to ensure the quality of incoming

materials and components.

Implementing Quality Management Principles:

To implement these principles effectively, organizations often follow a set of steps:

1. **Assessment:** Begin by assessing the organization's current state of quality management. Identify strengths and weaknesses.

2. **Leadership Commitment:** Ensure top leadership is committed to quality and willing to champion quality initiatives.

3. **Employee Engagement:** Involve employees in quality improvement efforts and provide training and resources.

4. **Process Mapping:** Map out key processes to identify areas for improvement and optimization.

5. **Data Collection and Analysis:** Use data to measure current performance, identify issues, and track progress.

6. **Continuous Improvement:** Develop a culture of continuous improvement where employees are encouraged to suggest and implement changes.

7. **Supplier Collaboration:** Strengthen relationships with suppliers, emphasizing quality and reliability.

8. **Feedback Loop:** Establish mechanisms for customer feedback and use it to drive improvements.

Conclusion:

Quality management principles serve as the foundation for organizations striving to achieve and maintain exceptional quality standards. They guide leaders, employees, and processes towards a shared vision of excellence, customer satisfaction, and continuous improvement. By adhering to these principles and integrating them into their culture and operations, organizations can consistently deliver superior products and services while fostering a culture of quality and excellence.

E. Benefits and Challenges of Quality Management

Quality management is a systematic approach that brings about numerous benefits for organizations. However, it is not without its challenges. Understanding both the advantages and potential obstacles is essential for organizations committed to implementing effective quality management.

Benefits of Quality Management:

1. **Improved Customer Satisfaction:** Meeting and exceeding customer expectations is at the core of quality management. When customers receive high-quality products and services,

their satisfaction increases, leading to loyalty, repeat business, and positive word-of-mouth referrals.

2. **Enhanced Reputation:** A strong commitment to quality enhances an organization's reputation in the marketplace. A positive reputation can attract more customers, partners, and opportunities for growth.

3. **Increased Efficiency:** Quality management promotes process optimization and efficiency. As processes become more streamlined and waste is reduced, organizations can operate more cost-effectively.

4. **Cost Reduction:** Quality management helps identify and eliminate errors, defects, and inefficiencies. This reduction in waste and rework leads to cost savings in the long run.

5. **Higher Productivity:** Engaged employees who understand and participate in quality management efforts tend to be more motivated and productive.

6. **Compliance and Risk Management:** Quality management often involves adherence to regulatory and industry standards. Compliance helps organizations avoid legal and financial risks.

7. **Innovation and Continuous Improvement:** A culture of quality encourages innovation and a focus on continuous

improvement. Organizations are more likely to identify and implement innovative solutions to problems.

8. **Strategic Advantage:** Organizations that excel in quality management gain a competitive edge. Quality can be a key differentiator in crowded markets.

9. **Better Decision Making:** Quality management emphasizes data-driven decision-making. Access to accurate data enables informed and strategic decision-making.

10. **Market Expansion:** Organizations with strong quality management practices may find it easier to enter new markets and gain the trust of international customers.

Challenges of Quality Management:

1. **Resistance to Change:** Implementing quality management often requires significant changes in processes and culture. Resistance to change from employees and management can hinder progress.

2. **Resource Intensive:** Establishing and maintaining a robust quality management system requires time, effort, and resources. Smaller organizations may find this particularly challenging.

3. **Complexity:** Quality management systems can become intricate, especially in large organizations with multiple

processes and locations. Managing this complexity can be daunting.

4. **Initial Investment:** There may be upfront costs associated with implementing quality management, including training, technology, and process improvements.

5. **Measuring Intangibles:** Some quality improvements, such as customer satisfaction and employee morale, are challenging to measure quantitatively.

6. **Resistance to Data:** Some employees may be resistant to data-driven decision-making or lack the necessary skills to analyze data effectively.

7. **Overemphasis on Metrics:** Overreliance on metrics without considering qualitative aspects of quality can lead to tunnel vision and neglect of important customer needs.

8. **Maintaining Momentum:** Achieving initial quality improvements is one thing; maintaining high standards over time can be a continuous challenge.

9. **Balancing Quality and Cost:** Organizations must strike a balance between quality improvement efforts and cost control. Overemphasizing one can lead to issues with the other.

10. **Supplier Quality:** Ensuring supplier quality can be a challenge, as it requires collaboration and quality assurance

throughout the supply chain.

Conclusion:

Quality management offers a multitude of benefits, ranging from customer satisfaction to cost reduction and strategic advantage. However, organizations must also navigate potential challenges related to change management, resource allocation, and complexity. By recognizing these challenges and proactively addressing them, organizations can maximize the benefits of quality management and achieve long-term success in delivering high-quality products and services.

CHAPTER 2

Introduction to Quality Management Frameworks

Quality management is a multifaceted discipline that encompasses various methodologies, principles, and practices aimed at achieving excellence and ensuring consistent quality in products, services, and processes. At the heart of effective quality management are the frameworks that provide structured approaches for organizations to plan, implement, and continually improve their quality efforts. In this section, we will explore the diverse landscape of quality management frameworks, each offering its own unique perspective and tools for achieving the highest standards of quality. These frameworks serve as invaluable guides for organizations across industries, helping them navigate the complex terrain of quality assurance and control.

A. ISO 9000 Series and Quality Standards

The International Organization for Standardization (ISO) 9000 series is arguably the most widely recognized and implemented set of quality standards globally. These standards provide a structured framework for establishing, implementing, and continually improving Quality Management Systems (QMS). ISO 9000 standards have become the benchmark for organizations seeking to demonstrate their commitment to quality, enhance customer satisfaction, and drive overall excellence.

ISO 9000 Series Overview:

The ISO 9000 series consists of several individual standards, with ISO 9001 being the most prominent. Each standard addresses specific aspects of quality management:

1. **ISO 9001: Quality Management Systems - Requirements:** ISO 9001 lays out the fundamental requirements for establishing and maintaining an effective QMS. Organizations that conform to ISO 9001 demonstrate their ability to consistently deliver products or services that meet customer requirements and regulatory standards. ISO 9001 certification is highly regarded and often required in various industries, making it a cornerstone of many quality management initiatives.

2. **ISO 9000: Quality Management Systems - Fundamentals and Vocabulary:** ISO 9000 provides essential terminology and concepts related to quality management. It serves as a foundational document for understanding the key principles and terminology used throughout the ISO 9000 series.

3. **ISO 9004: Quality Management - Quality of an Organization:** ISO 9004 complements ISO 9001 by offering guidelines for enhancing organizational performance beyond the minimum requirements. It focuses on achieving sustained success, customer satisfaction, and ongoing improvement.

4. **ISO 19011: Guidelines for Auditing Management Systems:** ISO 19011 provides guidelines for auditing management systems, including QMS. It is used to ensure that QMS conform to ISO 9001 requirements and are effectively implemented and maintained.

Key Concepts within ISO 9001:

ISO 9001 embodies several core concepts and principles that organizations must embrace to achieve certification and realize the benefits of a robust QMS:

1. **Process Approach:** ISO 9001 encourages organizations to view their activities as interconnected processes. This approach emphasizes the importance of understanding and managing these processes to achieve consistent and predictable quality outcomes. The Plan-Do-Check-Act (PDCA) cycle is often used to guide process improvement.

2. **Customer Focus:** ISO 9001 places significant emphasis on customer satisfaction. Organizations must determine and meet customer needs, monitor customer satisfaction, and use

customer feedback for continual improvement.

3. **Leadership and Commitment:** Top management plays a crucial role in implementing and sustaining a QMS. Leaders are expected to establish a clear quality policy, set objectives, allocate resources, and demonstrate their commitment to quality.

4. **Involvement of People:** Engaged employees are essential for the success of a QMS. ISO 9001 encourages organizations to involve employees, provide training, and create an environment where employees can contribute to quality improvement.

5. **Data-Driven Decision Making:** ISO 9001 promotes data-driven decision-making. Organizations are expected to collect and analyze relevant data to evaluate performance, identify areas for improvement, and make informed decisions.

Benefits of ISO 9000 Series:

Implementing the ISO 9000 series offers numerous advantages for organizations:

1. **Enhanced Quality:** ISO 9001 helps organizations establish a culture of quality and consistency, resulting in improved product and service quality.

2. **Increased Customer Satisfaction:** Customer focus is central

to ISO 9001, leading to higher customer satisfaction and loyalty.

3. **Operational Efficiency:** The process approach and continual improvement aspects of ISO 9001 can streamline operations, reduce waste, and boost efficiency.

4. **Global Recognition:** ISO 9001 certification is recognized worldwide, enhancing an organization's reputation and competitiveness.

5. **Risk Mitigation:** ISO 9001's focus on risk-based thinking helps organizations identify and address potential issues before they become major problems.

6. **Regulatory Compliance:** ISO 9001 can help organizations comply with industry-specific regulations and standards.

Challenges of ISO 9000 Series:

While ISO 9000 standards offer significant benefits, they also present challenges:

1. **Resource Requirements:** Implementing and maintaining a QMS can be resource-intensive, requiring time, personnel, and financial investments.

2. **Complexity:** Understanding and applying the standards' requirements can be complex, particularly for smaller

organizations or those new to quality management.

3. **Resistance to Change:** Employees and management may resist changes required to align with ISO 9001 standards.

4. **Certification Costs:** Achieving and maintaining ISO 9001 certification involves costs for audits, training, and documentation.

Conclusion:

The ISO 9000 series and ISO 9001, in particular, play a central role in the world of quality management. They provide a structured framework that helps organizations establish effective QMS, improve their operations, enhance customer satisfaction, and achieve global recognition. However, successful implementation requires commitment, resources, and a deep understanding of the standards' requirements. Organizations that navigate these challenges effectively often reap the substantial benefits of ISO 9000 certification.

B. Lean Six Sigma Methodology

Lean Six Sigma is a powerful and widely adopted methodology that combines the principles of Lean and Six Sigma to achieve process excellence, reduce waste, improve quality, and drive overall organizational efficiency. This methodology has proven to be particularly effective in various industries, including manufacturing, healthcare, finance, and service sectors.

Understanding Lean Six Sigma:

1. **Lean Principles:**

Value: Lean thinking starts with identifying what customers value in a product or service. Anything that does not directly contribute to this value is considered waste.

Waste Reduction: Lean focuses on eliminating waste in processes. The seven common types of waste identified in Lean are overproduction, waiting, unnecessary transportation, excess inventory, overprocessing, defects, and underutilized employee skills (often referred to as the "7 Wastes").

Continuous Flow: Lean seeks to create continuous and smooth flow in processes, minimizing interruptions and delays.

Pull Systems: Lean uses pull systems to align production or service delivery with actual demand. Work is initiated in response to customer demand, reducing excess inventory and overproduction.

Standardization: Standardized work processes and procedures are developed to ensure consistency and reduce variation.

2. Six Sigma Principles:

Data-Driven Decision-Making: Six Sigma emphasizes the use of statistical tools and data analysis to measure and improve processes.

Define, Measure, Analyze, Improve, Control (DMAIC): DMAIC is a structured problem-solving approach used in Six Sigma projects. It consists of five phases: Define the problem, Measure process performance, Analyze data, Improve the process, and Control process performance to maintain improvements.

Process Variation Reduction: Six Sigma focuses on reducing process variation to achieve consistent and predictable outcomes. The goal is to achieve a sigma level that indicates a high level of process capability and quality.

Customer-Centric: Six Sigma places a strong emphasis on understanding and meeting customer requirements.

The Lean Six Sigma Methodology:

Lean Six Sigma combines the principles of Lean and Six Sigma into a comprehensive methodology that integrates waste reduction (Lean) with statistical analysis and variation reduction (Six Sigma). The key components of Lean Six Sigma are:

1. **Define:** In this phase, the project goals and objectives are clearly defined, along with the problem or opportunity to be

addressed. The project scope is established, and the team is formed.

2. **Measure:** The Measure phase involves collecting data to quantify the current process performance. Process maps, data collection plans, and measurement systems analysis are utilized to ensure accurate data.

3. **Analyze:** During this phase, data analysis is conducted to identify root causes of problems or inefficiencies. Statistical tools and techniques are used to pinpoint areas for improvement.

4. **Improve:** In the Improve phase, potential solutions are generated, tested, and implemented. The focus is on making process changes that will result in measurable improvements.

5. **Control:** The Control phase ensures that the improvements are sustained over time. Control plans and monitoring mechanisms are put in place to prevent regression and maintain the gains.

Benefits of Lean Six Sigma:

1. **Waste Reduction:** Lean Six Sigma helps organizations identify and eliminate waste, reducing costs and improving efficiency.

2. **Quality Improvement:** The methodology focuses on reducing defects and process variation, leading to higher

product and service quality.

3. **Customer Satisfaction:** By aligning processes with customer needs and reducing errors, Lean Six Sigma often leads to increased customer satisfaction.

4. **Data-Driven Decision Making:** The emphasis on data analysis enhances decision-making based on facts rather than intuition.

5. **Improved Efficiency:** Lean principles lead to smoother process flows and reduced cycle times, improving overall operational efficiency.

6. **Cost Savings:** The reduction in waste, defects, and inefficiencies directly translates into cost savings for organizations.

7. **Competitive Advantage:** Organizations that embrace Lean Six Sigma often gain a competitive edge by delivering higher quality products and services more efficiently.

Challenges of Lean Six Sigma:

1. **Resource Intensive:** Implementing Lean Six Sigma requires dedicated resources, including training, project teams, and data analysis tools.

2. **Cultural Resistance:** Changing an organization's culture to

embrace Lean Six Sigma principles can be challenging and may face resistance from employees.

3. **Complexity:** The methodology can be complex, especially for organizations new to Lean Six Sigma.

4. **Initial Investment:** There may be upfront costs associated with training, process changes, and tools.

5. **Project Selection:** Identifying the right projects and prioritizing them can be a challenge.

Conclusion:

Lean Six Sigma is a dynamic methodology that brings together the best of Lean's waste reduction and efficiency focus with Six Sigma's data-driven problem-solving and quality improvement. When implemented effectively, Lean Six Sigma can drive significant improvements in quality, customer satisfaction, and operational efficiency, making it a valuable tool for organizations seeking to excel in today's competitive landscape.

C. Kaizen and Continuous Improvement

Kaizen, a Japanese term meaning "change for better" or "continuous improvement," is a philosophy and methodology that has had a profound impact on quality management and organizational excellence. Rooted in Japanese manufacturing,

Kaizen principles have been widely adopted across industries worldwide to drive incremental improvements in processes, products, and services. This section explores the principles of Kaizen and its application in achieving continuous improvement.

Understanding Kaizen:

Kaizen is founded on several core principles and practices that guide its application:

1. **Continuous Improvement:** At the heart of Kaizen is the commitment to ongoing, incremental improvement. It recognizes that small, consistent changes can lead to significant advancements over time.

2. **Customer Focus:** Kaizen emphasizes understanding and meeting customer needs and expectations. Customer feedback is a valuable source of information for identifying areas for improvement.

3. **Employee Involvement:** Employees are encouraged to actively participate in the improvement process. Their knowledge, experience, and creativity are tapped to identify and implement changes.

4. **Standardization:** Kaizen seeks to establish standardized work processes and procedures. This standardization ensures consistency and provides a basis for further improvement.

5. **Waste Reduction:** Similar to Lean principles, Kaizen aims to reduce waste in processes. The seven common types of waste identified in Lean (overproduction, waiting, unnecessary transportation, excess inventory, overprocessing, defects, and underutilized employee skills) are also relevant in Kaizen.

6. **PDCA Cycle:** The Plan-Do-Check-Act (PDCA) cycle is often used as a structured approach to continuous improvement in Kaizen. It involves planning changes, implementing them, checking their effectiveness, and acting on the results to make further improvements.

Kaizen Methodology:

Kaizen implementation typically involves the following steps:

1. **Identify Areas for Improvement:** Organizations identify processes, products, or services that need improvement. This can be done through customer feedback, employee suggestions, or performance metrics.

2. **Set Specific Goals:** Clear, measurable objectives are set for the improvement project. These goals provide direction and a basis for evaluating success.

3. **Analyze Current State:** The current state of the process or area under review is analyzed to identify bottlenecks, inefficiencies, and areas of waste.

4. **Generate Ideas:** Employees and teams brainstorm and generate ideas for improvement. No idea is too small, and creativity is encouraged.

5. **Implement Changes:** Selected improvements are put into practice. It's important to start with small changes that can be easily tested and refined.

6. **Measure Results:** Key performance indicators (KPIs) are monitored to assess the impact of the changes. Data is collected and analyzed to determine whether the improvements have been effective.

7. **Standardize and Sustain:** Once successful changes are identified, they are standardized to become part of the standard operating procedures. Additionally, the organization strives to maintain the culture of continuous improvement.

Benefits of Kaizen:

1. **Incremental Improvements:** Kaizen's focus on small, frequent improvements leads to steady progress over time.

2. **Employee Engagement:** Involving employees in the improvement process fosters a sense of ownership and engagement.

3. **Cost Reduction:** Identifying and eliminating waste leads to cost savings.

4. **Quality Improvement:** Continuous monitoring and improvement often result in higher product and service quality.

5. **Efficiency Gains:** Streamlining processes and reducing bottlenecks improves operational efficiency.

6. **Customer Satisfaction:** By addressing customer concerns and needs, Kaizen can enhance customer satisfaction.

7. **Cultural Transformation:** Kaizen can instill a culture of continuous improvement within an organization.

Challenges of Kaizen:

1. **Resource and Time Intensive:** Effective Kaizen requires dedicated resources, time, and a commitment to ongoing improvement.

2. **Resistance to Change:** Employees and management may resist changes to established processes.

3. **Measurement Challenges:** Identifying and measuring the impact of incremental changes can be challenging.

4. **Sustainability:** Sustaining a culture of continuous improvement over the long term requires ongoing effort and commitment.

Conclusion:

Kaizen is a powerful philosophy and methodology for achieving continuous improvement in organizations. It emphasizes incremental, employee-driven changes that lead to enhanced quality, efficiency, and customer satisfaction. While implementing Kaizen may pose challenges, the benefits of fostering a culture of continuous improvement often far outweigh the efforts invested. Kaizen's principles continue to shape the landscape of quality management and organizational excellence worldwide.

D. TQM Principles and Practices

Total Quality Management (TQM) is a comprehensive approach to quality that permeates an organization from top to bottom. It encompasses principles, practices, and strategies aimed at achieving excellence, enhancing customer satisfaction, and continuously improving processes, products, and services. TQM has evolved over the years, and this section explores its foundational principles and key components.

Understanding Total Quality Management:

TQM is rooted in several fundamental principles and practices that guide its implementation:

1. **Customer Focus:**

- TQM begins with a deep understanding of customer needs and expectations. Organizations must listen to their customers, gather feedback, and use it to drive improvements.

- The ultimate goal is to not only meet but exceed customer expectations, which fosters loyalty and positive word-of-mouth referrals.

2. **Continuous Improvement:**

- A cornerstone of TQM is the belief that processes and products can always be improved. The pursuit of excellence is ongoing, and organizations must commit to continuous improvement.

- The Plan-Do-Check-Act (PDCA) cycle is often used to guide TQM's continuous improvement efforts.

3. **Employee Involvement and Empowerment:**

- Employees are considered invaluable assets in TQM. They possess knowledge, skills, and insights that can contribute to quality improvement.

- TQM encourages employee involvement in decision-making, problem-solving, and the overall quality improvement process.

- Empowered employees have the authority to make decisions

and take actions that enhance quality.

4. **Process-Centric Approach:**

- TQM promotes a process-centric view of an organization. It involves mapping and analyzing processes to identify areas for improvement.

- Processes are continually monitored, measured, and optimized to achieve consistent quality outcomes.

5. **Data-Driven Decision Making:**

- TQM relies on data and measurement to make informed decisions. Statistical tools and analysis are used to monitor processes, identify variations, and drive improvements.

- Data provides the evidence needed to assess the effectiveness of quality initiatives and make necessary adjustments.

6. **Supplier Relationships:**

- TQM recognizes the importance of supplier quality. Organizations work closely with suppliers to ensure the quality of incoming materials and components.

- Collaborative relationships with suppliers help prevent defects and improve overall product quality.

7. Leadership and Commitment:

- Strong leadership is essential for successful TQM implementation. Leaders set the vision, create a culture of quality, and provide the necessary resources for quality improvement.

- Leadership commitment to TQM is demonstrated through active involvement, support for employee initiatives, and the allocation of time and resources.

8. Strategic Alignment:

- TQM aligns quality objectives with the organization's strategic goals. Quality becomes an integral part of the business strategy.

- Strategic alignment ensures that quality initiatives are prioritized and supported at all levels of the organization.

9. Prevention over Inspection:

- TQM emphasizes preventing defects and problems rather than relying solely on inspection and correction after the fact.

- The focus is on addressing root causes and building quality into processes from the outset.

Implementing Total Quality Management:

Implementing TQM effectively involves several key steps:

1. **Assessment:** Begin with an assessment of the organization's current quality management practices, culture, and performance. Identify strengths, weaknesses, and areas for improvement.

2. **Leadership Commitment:** Ensure top leadership is fully committed to TQM and actively champions quality initiatives.

3. **Employee Engagement:** Involve employees in quality improvement efforts, provide training, and create a culture where employees feel empowered to contribute.

4. **Process Mapping:** Map out key processes to identify bottlenecks, inefficiencies, and areas for improvement.

5. **Data Collection and Analysis:** Use data to measure current performance, identify issues, and track progress toward quality goals.

6. **Continuous Improvement:** Foster a culture of continuous improvement where employees are encouraged to suggest and implement changes.

7. **Supplier Collaboration:** Strengthen relationships with suppliers, emphasizing quality and reliability.

8. **Feedback Loop:** Establish mechanisms for customer feedback and use it to drive improvements.

Benefits of Total Quality Management:

Implementing TQM yields numerous benefits for organizations:

1. **Improved Quality:** TQM leads to higher product and service quality, resulting in fewer defects and customer complaints.

2. **Increased Customer Satisfaction:** A focus on customer needs and continuous improvement enhances customer satisfaction and loyalty.

3. **Enhanced Efficiency:** Streamlined processes and reduced waste improve operational efficiency.

4. **Cost Reduction:** TQM helps identify and eliminate waste, leading to cost savings.

5. **Competitive Advantage:** Organizations that excel in TQM often gain a competitive edge in the marketplace.

6. **Risk Mitigation:** TQM's focus on prevention helps organizations avoid costly defects and errors.

7. **Innovation:** A culture of continuous improvement encourages innovative thinking and problem-solving.

Challenges of Total Quality Management:

While TQM offers significant advantages, it also presents challenges:

1. **Resource Intensive:** Implementing and sustaining TQM requires dedicated resources, including time, personnel, and financial investments.

2. **Cultural Change:** Changing the organizational culture to embrace TQM principles can be challenging and may face resistance from employees.

3. **Complexity:** TQM can be complex, especially for organizations new to quality management.

4. **Initial Investment:** Achieving and maintaining TQM requires upfront costs for training, process changes, and tools.

5. **Balancing Quality and Cost:** Organizations must strike a balance between quality improvement efforts and cost control.

Conclusion:

Total Quality Management is a holistic approach to quality that emphasizes customer focus, continuous improvement, employee involvement, and data-driven decision-making. When implemented effectively, TQM helps organizations deliver high-quality products and services, enhance customer satisfaction, and gain a competitive advantage. While it may present challenges, organizations that commit to TQM often reap the substantial rewards of sustained quality excellence.

E. Baldrige Excellence Framework

The Baldrige Excellence Framework, often referred to simply as the Baldrige Framework, is a comprehensive and highly respected quality management framework used in the United States. Named after Malcolm Baldrige Jr., a former U.S. Secretary of Commerce, this framework provides a systematic approach to achieving organizational excellence and performance improvement. It serves as a valuable resource for organizations across sectors, including healthcare, education, manufacturing, and service industries.

Understanding the Baldrige Excellence Framework:

The Baldrige Excellence Framework is built upon several key principles and criteria that guide organizations toward achieving excellence:

1. Leadership:

- The framework emphasizes the critical role of leadership in shaping an organization's culture, setting strategic directions, and ensuring sustainability.

- Leaders are expected to create a clear vision, engage employees, and promote ethical behavior and transparency.

2. **Strategy:**

- Organizations must develop and execute effective strategies to achieve their goals and fulfill their mission.

- Strategic planning, alignment, and deployment are essential components of this criterion.

3. **Customers:**

- Understanding and engaging customers are central to the Baldrige Framework. Organizations must identify their customer segments, gather feedback, and continuously improve customer satisfaction.

- Customer-focused measures and feedback mechanisms are integral to this criterion.

4. **Measurement, Analysis, and Knowledge Management:**

- Data-driven decision-making is a fundamental principle. Organizations are expected to collect, analyze, and use data effectively to drive performance improvement.

- Knowledge management practices ensure that organizational knowledge is captured, shared, and used for continuous learning.

5. **Workforce:**

- Employees are considered key stakeholders in organizational success. Effective workforce management includes talent acquisition, development, engagement, and satisfaction.

- Learning and development programs and employee involvement in decision-making are essential elements.

6. **Operations:**

- Efficient and effective operations are crucial for delivering value to customers. Organizations must focus on process management, performance measurement, and innovation.

- Supply chain management and waste reduction are also emphasized.

7. **Results:**

- The ultimate criterion assesses organizational performance and results. It evaluates outcomes related to customers, employees, finances, operations, and community engagement.

- Results are measured using a variety of performance indicators.

Implementing the Baldrige Excellence Framework:

To implement the Baldrige Framework effectively,

organizations typically follow a set of steps:

1. **Self-Assessment:** Organizations begin by conducting a self-assessment against the Baldrige criteria. This helps identify strengths and areas for improvement.

2. **Development of Improvement Plans:** Based on the self-assessment, organizations develop improvement plans and initiatives to address identified gaps.

3. **Implementation:** Improvement initiatives are implemented across the organization. This often involves cross-functional teams and a focus on data-driven decision-making.

4. **Monitoring and Measurement:** Organizations continually monitor and measure performance using relevant metrics and indicators. Data analysis is used to assess the effectiveness of improvement efforts.

5. **Feedback and Adjustment:** The Baldrige Framework encourages organizations to seek feedback from stakeholders and adjust their strategies and processes accordingly.

6. **Application for Awards (Optional):** Some organizations choose to apply for the Malcolm Baldrige National Quality Award, a prestigious recognition in the U.S. that acknowledges organizations demonstrating excellence. The application process involves a rigorous evaluation by Baldrige

examiners.

Benefits of the Baldrige Excellence Framework:

1. **Performance Excellence:** The Baldrige Framework provides a structured approach to achieving excellence in all aspects of an organization's operations.

2. **Organizational Learning:** The framework encourages a culture of learning and continuous improvement.

3. **Stakeholder Engagement:** Emphasis on customers and employees fosters strong stakeholder engagement.

4. **Strategic Alignment:** The Baldrige criteria ensure that organizational strategies are aligned with its mission and goals.

5. **Data-Driven Decision Making:** Data collection and analysis are central to the framework, promoting informed decision-making.

6. **Competitive Advantage:** Organizations that excel in implementing the Baldrige Framework often gain a competitive edge in their industries.

Challenges of the Baldrige Excellence Framework:

1. **Resource Intensive:** Implementing the framework requires dedicated resources, including time, personnel, and financial

investments.

2. **Complexity:** The Baldrige criteria can be intricate, and organizations may need assistance in interpreting and applying them effectively.

3. **Cultural Transformation:** Shifting an organization's culture to fully embrace the Baldrige principles may face resistance.

4. **Measuring Impact:** Quantifying the impact of Baldrige-based improvements can be challenging.

Conclusion:

The Baldrige Excellence Framework is a robust and widely recognized quality management framework that offers a structured path to organizational excellence. By focusing on leadership, strategy, customers, measurement, and results, organizations can drive performance improvement, enhance stakeholder engagement, and gain a competitive advantage. While implementing the Baldrige Framework presents challenges, the benefits of achieving excellence and sustainability make it a valuable resource for organizations committed to quality and performance excellence.

F. Comparing Quality Frameworks

In the diverse landscape of quality management, organizations have several frameworks and methodologies to choose from, each offering unique approaches to achieving excellence, enhancing customer satisfaction, and ensuring quality in products and services. This section will delve into the comparative analysis of some of the prominent quality frameworks, including ISO 9000, Lean Six Sigma, Total Quality Management (TQM), and the Baldrige Excellence Framework.

ISO 9000 vs. Lean Six Sigma vs. TQM vs. Baldrige:

1. **ISO 9000 Series:**

- **Focus:** ISO 9000 primarily focuses on establishing and maintaining Quality Management Systems (QMS) to meet customer requirements and enhance product and service quality.

- **Scope:** ISO 9000 is applicable to a wide range of industries and organizations seeking to achieve international recognition for their commitment to quality.

- **Methodology:** ISO 9000 emphasizes compliance with a set of standards and guidelines. It provides a structured framework for documenting processes, setting quality objectives, and continuous improvement.

- **Benefits:** ISO 9000 certification is globally recognized and can enhance an organization's reputation, improve customer satisfaction, and promote regulatory compliance.

- **Challenges:** Implementing ISO 9000 can be resource-intensive, and some organizations may struggle with the complexity of the standards.

2. **Lean Six Sigma:**

- **Focus:** Lean Six Sigma combines the principles of Lean (waste reduction) and Six Sigma (variation reduction) to improve process efficiency and product/service quality.

- **Scope:** Lean Six Sigma is widely applied in manufacturing, healthcare, finance, and service industries where process optimization and quality improvement are critical.

- **Methodology:** Lean Six Sigma employs the DMAIC (Define, Measure, Analyze, Improve, Control) or DMADV (Define, Measure, Analyze, Design, Verify) methodology for structured problem-solving and process improvement.

- **Benefits:** Lean Six Sigma is known for delivering rapid and measurable results, including reduced defects, cost savings, and enhanced customer satisfaction.

- **Challenges:** Implementing Lean Six Sigma may require significant training and resources. Some organizations find it challenging to maintain a focus on continuous improvement.

3. Total Quality Management (TQM):

- **Focus:** TQM is a holistic approach to quality that emphasizes customer satisfaction, employee involvement, and continuous improvement in all aspects of an organization.

- **Scope:** TQM can be applied across various industries and is particularly suited for organizations seeking a cultural transformation toward quality excellence.

- **Methodology:** TQM relies on principles such as customer focus, leadership commitment, process improvement, employee empowerment, and data-driven decision-making.

- **Benefits:** TQM fosters a culture of continuous improvement, leading to higher quality, increased customer satisfaction, and enhanced operational efficiency.

- **Challenges:** Implementing TQM requires a significant cultural shift and leadership commitment. It can be resource-intensive in terms of training and change management.

4. Baldrige Excellence Framework:

- **Focus:** The Baldrige Framework promotes organizational excellence by assessing leadership, strategy, customers, measurement, workforce, operations, and results.

- **Scope:** The Baldrige Framework is widely used in the United

States, particularly in healthcare, education, and service industries, to drive organizational excellence.

- **Methodology:** The framework provides a structured set of criteria and principles that guide organizations toward performance excellence, sustainability, and continuous improvement.

- **Benefits:** Organizations that excel in implementing the Baldrige Framework often gain recognition for excellence and a competitive advantage in their industries.

- **Challenges:** Implementing the Baldrige Framework can be complex, and organizations may require assistance in interpreting and applying its criteria effectively.

Comparative Analysis:

- **Scope:** ISO 9000 is a globally recognized standard applicable to a broad range of industries. Lean Six Sigma is widely used in various sectors, with a focus on process optimization. TQM and the Baldrige Framework are often favored by organizations seeking holistic cultural transformations.

- **Methodology:** ISO 9000 relies on compliance with standards. Lean Six Sigma follows a structured DMAIC/DMADV methodology. TQM emphasizes principles like customer focus and employee involvement. The Baldrige Framework offers a comprehensive set of criteria.

- **Benefits:** ISO 9000 offers international recognition and regulatory compliance. Lean Six Sigma delivers rapid results and cost savings. TQM fosters a culture of continuous improvement. The Baldrige Framework promotes excellence and recognition.

- **Challenges:** ISO 9000 may require significant resources. Lean Six Sigma needs ongoing focus. TQM demands cultural change. The Baldrige Framework can be complex.

Selection Considerations:

- Organizations should select a framework based on their industry, goals, culture, and resources.

- ISO 9000 suits organizations seeking international recognition and regulatory compliance.

- Lean Six Sigma is ideal for rapid improvements and cost savings.

- TQM is suitable for cultural transformations and holistic quality excellence.

- The Baldrige Framework is valuable for organizations aiming for performance excellence and recognition.

In summary, each quality framework has its unique strengths

and applicability. The choice of framework should align with an organization's strategic objectives, culture, and specific quality improvement needs. Many organizations even combine elements from multiple frameworks to create a customized approach that suits their unique circumstances and goals.

CHAPTER 3

Quality Planning and Strategy

Quality Planning and Strategy are fundamental components of effective quality management. In the journey towards delivering superior products and services, organizations must meticulously plan and strategically align their processes to meet customer expectations and achieve their quality objectives. This chapter explores the pivotal role of Quality Planning and Strategy in ensuring that an organization's quality efforts are well-directed and yield tangible results. From defining quality policies and objectives to employing strategic tools and metrics, this chapter delves into the intricacies of crafting and executing a quality-focused roadmap for success.

A. Quality Policy and Objectives

Quality Policy and Objectives are crucial elements in the Quality Planning and Strategy of any organization committed to delivering high-quality products or services. These components help define the organization's quality aspirations, provide a clear sense of direction, and serve as a foundation for the development of effective quality management systems. In this section, we will delve into the in-depth understanding of Quality Policy and Objectives, their significance, and their role in achieving overall quality excellence.

Quality Policy:

Definition: A Quality Policy is a formal statement or declaration by an organization that outlines its commitment to delivering quality and meeting customer requirements. It serves as a guiding principle for the organization's quality-related activities and reflects its overall quality culture and values.

Key Components of a Quality Policy:

1. **Commitment to Quality:** The policy should emphasize the organization's unwavering commitment to providing high-quality products or services.

2. **Customer Focus:** It should underline the organization's dedication to meeting or exceeding customer expectations.

3. **Applicability:** The policy should specify to whom it applies, typically to all employees, contractors, and stakeholders involved in the organization's activities.

4. **Compliance:** Mentioning adherence to relevant quality standards, regulations, and requirements is often part of the policy.

5. **Continuous Improvement:** Highlighting the organization's commitment to continuous improvement and innovation in quality processes.

6. **Responsibility:** Defining roles and responsibilities for maintaining and implementing the quality policy.

Importance of a Quality Policy:

- **Guiding Principle:** A Quality Policy provides a guiding principle for employees at all levels, ensuring everyone is aligned with the organization's quality objectives.

- **Customer Confidence:** It instills confidence in customers, demonstrating the organization's dedication to delivering products or services of consistent quality.

- **Legal and Regulatory Compliance:** The policy helps ensure that the organization complies with relevant quality standards and regulations.

- **Decision-Making:** It aids in decision-making by providing a clear framework for quality-related choices.

- **Employee Engagement:** A well-communicated quality policy engages employees and encourages their active involvement in quality improvement efforts.

Quality Objectives:

Definition: Quality Objectives are specific, measurable, and time-bound targets set by an organization to achieve its quality-related goals. These objectives should be aligned with the organization's Quality Policy and strategic direction.

Characteristics of Quality Objectives:

1. **Specific:** Objectives should be clear and unambiguous, leaving no room for misinterpretation.

2. **Measurable:** There should be quantifiable criteria to evaluate whether an objective has been achieved.

3. **Achievable:** Objectives should be realistic and attainable within the specified timeframe.

4. **Relevant:** Objectives should align with the organization's Quality Policy and contribute to its overall quality goals.

5. **Time-Bound:** Each objective should have a defined timeframe or deadline for accomplishment.

Examples of Quality Objectives:

1. **Reduce Defect Rate:** Decrease the defect rate in the manufacturing process by 20% within the next six months.

2. **Improve Customer Satisfaction:** Increase the customer

satisfaction index score by 10 points over the next year.

3. **Enhance Supplier Performance:** Achieve a 95% on-time delivery rate from suppliers within the next quarter.

4. **Reduce Turnaround Time:** Decrease the average customer support response time from 24 hours to 12 hours within three months.

Significance of Quality Objectives:

- **Performance Measurement:** Quality Objectives serve as benchmarks for measuring performance and progress toward quality goals.

- **Focus and Prioritization:** They help organizations prioritize their quality improvement efforts by highlighting specific areas that require attention.

- **Motivation:** Clearly defined and achievable objectives motivate employees and teams to strive for excellence.

- **Accountability:** Setting objectives creates a sense of accountability for results and encourages individuals and teams to take ownership of quality-related tasks.

- **Continuous Improvement:** Objectives drive a culture of continuous improvement, fostering innovation and adaptability.

In summary, a well-crafted Quality Policy and clear Quality Objectives are essential components of an organization's Quality Planning and Strategy. They provide a roadmap for quality-related activities, ensure alignment with organizational goals, and promote a culture of quality excellence. When effectively communicated and integrated into an organization's operations, these elements play a pivotal role in achieving and sustaining superior quality standards and customer satisfaction.

B. Quality Planning Tools (QFD, FMEA)

Quality Planning Tools are essential instruments in the arsenal of organizations striving to deliver superior products or services while systematically managing risk and ensuring customer satisfaction. Among these tools, Quality Function Deployment (QFD) and Failure Mode and Effects Analysis (FMEA) stand out as invaluable methodologies for effective quality planning. In this section, we will explore these tools in-depth, understanding their principles, methodologies, and applications in detail.

Quality Function Deployment (QFD):

Definition: Quality Function Deployment (QFD) is a structured approach that translates customer needs and requirements into specific product or service features and characteristics. It is a systematic process that aligns the entire organization with the voice of the customer, facilitating the design and development of products or services that truly meet customer expectations.

Key Components of QFD:

1. **Customer Requirements:** QFD begins by capturing and prioritizing customer requirements, which can be both explicit (stated by the customer) and implicit (not directly expressed but inferred from customer feedback).

2. **House of Quality:** The central tool in QFD is the House of Quality, a matrix that correlates customer requirements with specific product or service characteristics. It helps identify the relationship between customer needs and the technical requirements that must be met.

3. **Technical Requirements:** Technical experts contribute by defining the technical requirements necessary to fulfill customer needs. These requirements often involve engineering and design specifications.

4. **Priority Ratings:** Priority ratings are assigned to indicate the importance of each technical requirement in meeting customer needs. These ratings guide decision-making and resource allocation.

5. **Interactions and Relationships:** The House of Quality also highlights interactions and relationships between technical

requirements, helping ensure that changes in one requirement do not adversely affect others.

Benefits of QFD:

- **Customer-Centric:** QFD ensures that products or services are designed and developed with a deep understanding of customer needs and preferences.

- **Cross-Functional Collaboration:** It encourages collaboration between different departments and teams within an organization, fostering a holistic approach to quality planning.

- **Risk Mitigation:** By identifying potential conflicts and risks early in the design phase, QFD helps prevent costly defects and design flaws.

- **Improved Decision-Making:** The prioritization of technical requirements and the clear mapping of customer needs aid in informed decision-making.

Failure Mode and Effects Analysis (FMEA):

Definition: Failure Mode and Effects Analysis (FMEA) is a systematic methodology for evaluating and mitigating potential failure modes in products, processes, or systems. FMEA helps organizations proactively identify and address vulnerabilities to prevent or minimize the impact of failures.

Key Steps in FMEA:

1. **Identify Failure Modes:** The first step involves identifying all possible failure modes - ways in which a product, process, or system can fail.

2. **Determine Effects:** For each failure mode, assess the potential effects on the product, process, or system. Consider customer impact, safety concerns, and regulatory compliance.

3. **Assign Severity Ratings:** Assign a severity rating to each failure mode, indicating the potential seriousness of its effects. Higher ratings denote more severe consequences.

4. **Identify Causes and Detection Methods:** Determine the causes of each failure mode and assess the likelihood of detecting these failure modes before they reach the customer. Assign ratings for both.

5. **Calculate Risk Priority Numbers (RPN):** The Risk Priority Number (RPN) is calculated by multiplying the severity, occurrence, and detection ratings. This number helps prioritize which failure modes require immediate attention.

6. **Prioritize Actions:** Based on RPN values, prioritize the failure modes for corrective actions. High-RPN items are addressed first to reduce risk.

7. **Implement Corrective Actions:** Develop and implement

actions to reduce the occurrence and improve detection of high-risk failure modes. Reevaluate the RPN after corrective actions are taken.

Benefits of FMEA:

- **Risk Reduction:** FMEA identifies and prioritizes potential failures, enabling organizations to take proactive measures to reduce the risk of these failures occurring.

- **Cost Savings:** By preventing defects and failures, organizations can save significant costs associated with rework, recalls, and customer complaints.

- **Quality Improvement:** FMEA fosters a culture of quality improvement by encouraging organizations to continuously assess and enhance their processes and products.

- **Customer Satisfaction:** Fewer product failures lead to improved customer satisfaction and loyalty.

- **Regulatory Compliance:** FMEA helps organizations meet regulatory requirements by identifying and addressing potential compliance issues.

Comparative Analysis:

- **Focus:** QFD focuses on aligning product or service features with customer needs and preferences. FMEA, on the other hand, concentrates on identifying and mitigating potential failures and their consequences.

- **Application Stage:** QFD is typically applied during the product or service design and development phase. FMEA can be applied at various stages, from design to manufacturing to process improvement.

- **Tools and Outputs:** QFD relies on the House of Quality and prioritized technical requirements. FMEA utilizes risk assessment matrices and RPN values to prioritize actions.

- **Purpose:** QFD aims to ensure that the final product or service meets customer expectations. FMEA aims to minimize risks and prevent failures in processes, products, or systems.

- **Cross-Functional Collaboration:** Both QFD and FMEA encourage collaboration among different teams and departments within an organization.

In summary, Quality Function Deployment (QFD) and Failure Mode and Effects Analysis (FMEA) are powerful quality planning tools with distinct purposes and methodologies. QFD aligns product or service features with customer needs, fostering customer-centric design. FMEA, on the other hand, proactively identifies and mitigates potential failures, reducing risks and enhancing overall quality. Organizations often use these tools in tandem to ensure both customer satisfaction and robust risk management.

C. Quality Metrics and Key Performance Indicators (KPIs)

Quality Metrics and Key Performance Indicators (KPIs) are indispensable tools in the arsenal of organizations committed to achieving and maintaining superior product and service quality. These measurement systems provide valuable insights into an organization's performance, help identify areas for improvement, and ensure that quality objectives are met. In this section, we will explore in-depth the concepts of Quality Metrics and KPIs, their significance, and their role in driving quality excellence.

Quality Metrics:

Definition: Quality Metrics are quantitative or qualitative measures used to assess the performance, effectiveness, and efficiency of processes, products, or services. These metrics provide a means to monitor quality-related activities, identify trends, and make data-driven decisions.

Characteristics of Quality Metrics:

1. **Relevance:** Metrics should be directly related to the organization's quality objectives and aligned with customer requirements.

2. **Measurability:** Metrics must be quantifiable or observable, making it possible to collect data consistently.

3. **Consistency:** Metrics should be defined and measured consistently over time to track changes and improvements.

4. **Actionability:** Metrics should provide actionable insights, allowing organizations to take corrective actions when necessary.

5. **Timeliness:** Data collection and reporting should be timely to support real-time decision-making.

Examples of Quality Metrics:

1. **Defect Rate:** The number of defects in a product or process divided by the total number of units or activities.

2. **Customer Satisfaction Score:** Surveys or feedback mechanisms used to measure customer satisfaction levels.

3. **On-Time Delivery Performance:** The percentage of products or services delivered to customers on or before the agreed-upon delivery date.

4. **First-Pass Yield (FPY):** The percentage of products or processes that meet quality standards without requiring rework or corrections.

5. **Cycle Time:** The time it takes to complete a specific process

or task.

6. **Return on Investment (ROI):** The financial return generated from quality improvement initiatives relative to the resources invested.

Benefits of Quality Metrics:

- **Performance Assessment:** Metrics provide an objective way to assess the performance of processes, products, or services.

- **Continuous Improvement:** They help identify areas for improvement and measure the effectiveness of quality enhancement initiatives.

- **Data-Driven Decisions:** Metrics support informed decision-making by providing quantifiable evidence.

- **Goal Alignment:** Metrics ensure alignment with quality objectives and customer requirements.

Key Performance Indicators (KPIs):

Definition: Key Performance Indicators (KPIs) are a subset of quality metrics that are particularly critical to an organization's strategic goals and performance. KPIs are carefully selected based on their direct relevance to overall business objectives.

Characteristics of KPIs:

1. **Strategic Alignment:** KPIs align with the organization's strategic goals and objectives.

2. **Focus:** KPIs are a focused set of metrics that highlight critical areas of performance.

3. **Actionable:** KPIs provide actionable insights, prompting organizations to take specific actions to achieve desired outcomes.

4. **Benchmarking:** KPIs often involve benchmarking against industry standards or competitors' performance.

5. **Visual Presentation:** KPIs are often presented visually, such as through dashboards, scorecards, or performance reports.

Examples of KPIs:

1. **Customer Retention Rate:** The percentage of customers retained over a specific period.

2. **Revenue Growth:** The increase in revenue compared to a previous period.

3. **Employee Satisfaction Index:** A measure of employee satisfaction and engagement.

4. **Net Promoter Score (NPS):** A metric that assesses customer

loyalty and willingness to recommend the organization to others.

5. **Cost of Quality (CoQ):** The total costs associated with achieving and maintaining quality, including prevention, appraisal, and failure costs.

6. **Supplier Performance Score:** An evaluation of supplier performance in meeting quality and delivery standards.

Benefits of KPIs:

- **Strategic Focus:** KPIs ensure that organizational efforts are concentrated on the most critical areas of performance.

- **Goal Tracking:** They help track progress toward strategic goals and provide early warning signals if objectives are not being met.

- **Decision-Making:** KPIs facilitate data-driven decision-making at the strategic level of the organization.

- **Accountability:** KPIs hold individuals and teams accountable for achieving strategic goals.

- **Performance Communication:** KPIs provide a concise way to communicate performance to stakeholders.

Comparative Analysis:

- **Scope:** Quality Metrics cover a wide range of measures used to assess quality-related activities. KPIs are a subset of metrics that focus on critical performance areas aligned with strategic goals.

- **Purpose:** Quality Metrics are used for monitoring and improvement across various aspects of quality. KPIs are specifically chosen to drive performance toward strategic objectives.

- **Relevance:** While both metrics and KPIs should be relevant, KPIs have a stronger strategic alignment and are directly linked to an organization's overarching goals.

- **Actionability:** Both metrics and KPIs should provide actionable insights, but KPIs, by definition, are highly actionable and tied to strategic initiatives.

In summary, Quality Metrics and Key Performance Indicators (KPIs) are indispensable tools for organizations striving to achieve and sustain high-quality products and services. Metrics provide a comprehensive view of quality-related activities, while KPIs enable organizations to focus on critical performance areas aligned with strategic goals. By leveraging these measurement systems effectively, organizations can drive continuous improvement, make informed decisions, and achieve excellence in quality and customer satisfaction.

D. Strategic Quality Management

Strategic Quality Management (SQM) is a comprehensive approach that integrates the principles of quality management into an organization's overarching strategic objectives. SQM aligns quality initiatives with the organization's mission, vision, and long-term goals, ensuring that quality becomes an integral part of its strategic planning and execution. In this section, we will explore Strategic Quality Management in-depth, including its principles, methodologies, and its role in achieving sustained quality excellence.

Principles of Strategic Quality Management:

1. **Alignment with Strategic Objectives:** SQM starts with aligning quality goals and initiatives with the organization's strategic objectives. This ensures that quality efforts contribute directly to the achievement of broader business goals.

2. **Customer Focus:** SQM emphasizes a customer-centric approach, where understanding and meeting customer needs are central to the organization's strategic decisions.

3. **Leadership Commitment:** Top leadership plays a critical

role in SQM by demonstrating unwavering commitment to quality, setting the tone for a quality-focused culture, and providing the necessary resources.

4. **Continuous Improvement:** SQM fosters a culture of continuous improvement by encouraging employees at all levels to identify opportunities for quality enhancement and innovation.

5. **Data-Driven Decision-Making:** SQM relies on data and metrics to drive informed decision-making. Key Performance Indicators (KPIs) are often central to SQM initiatives.

6. **Employee Involvement:** Engaging employees in quality improvement initiatives and decision-making is a fundamental aspect of SQM. Employees are seen as valuable contributors to the quality process.

7. **Process Orientation:** SQM places a strong emphasis on understanding and optimizing processes to enhance quality and efficiency.

Methodologies and Tools in Strategic Quality Management:

1. **Balanced Scorecard:** The Balanced Scorecard is a popular tool in SQM that translates an organization's strategic objectives into a set of balanced KPIs. It helps monitor

performance across various dimensions, including financial, customer, internal processes, and learning and growth.

2. **Hoshin Kanri (Policy Deployment):** Hoshin Kanri is a Japanese approach to strategic planning and deployment. It involves setting clear strategic objectives, cascading them throughout the organization, and ensuring alignment and execution at all levels.

3. **SWOT Analysis:** SWOT (Strengths, Weaknesses, Opportunities, Threats) analysis is used in SQM to assess the organization's internal strengths and weaknesses and external opportunities and threats. It helps inform strategic decisions.

4. **Quality Function Deployment (QFD):** As discussed earlier, QFD helps align product or service features with customer needs, making it a valuable tool for SQM.

Steps in Implementing Strategic Quality Management:

1. **Strategic Assessment:** Begin with a thorough assessment of the organization's current strategic position, including its strengths, weaknesses, opportunities, and threats. Identify strategic objectives.

2. **Quality Goal Setting:** Define quality goals and objectives that align with the broader strategic objectives. These goals should be Specific, Measurable, Achievable, Relevant, and Time-

bound (SMART).

3. **KPI Development:** Establish Key Performance Indicators (KPIs) that directly measure progress toward quality and strategic goals. These KPIs should provide actionable insights.

4. **Resource Allocation:** Allocate the necessary resources, including personnel, budget, and technology, to support quality initiatives and strategic execution.

5. **Execution and Monitoring:** Implement quality improvement initiatives and monitor performance against established KPIs. Regularly review progress and make necessary adjustments.

6. **Continuous Improvement:** Encourage a culture of continuous improvement by capturing lessons learned and best practices, and incorporating them into future strategies.

Benefits of Strategic Quality Management:

1. **Alignment:** SQM ensures that quality initiatives are closely aligned with strategic goals, maximizing their impact on overall performance.

2. **Improved Decision-Making:** Data-driven decision-making supported by KPIs leads to more informed choices that drive quality and strategic success.

3. **Enhanced Customer Satisfaction:** SQM's customer-centric

approach results in products and services that better meet customer needs, leading to increased satisfaction and loyalty.

4. **Efficiency and Effectiveness:** Optimized processes and resource allocation increase efficiency and effectiveness in achieving strategic and quality goals.

5. **Competitive Advantage:** Organizations practicing SQM often gain a competitive edge by consistently delivering high-quality products or services.

6. **Adaptability:** SQM fosters a culture of adaptability and innovation, allowing organizations to respond effectively to changing market conditions.

Challenges of Strategic Quality Management:

1. **Resource Constraints:** Implementing SQM may require significant investments in terms of time, personnel, and financial resources.

2. **Cultural Change:** Shifting an organization's culture to embrace SQM principles can be challenging and may face resistance.

3. **Complexity:** Balancing strategic goals with quality objectives can be complex, requiring careful planning and execution.

4. **Measuring Impact:** Quantifying the impact of SQM

initiatives on strategic outcomes can be difficult, as some improvements may take time to materialize.

In conclusion, Strategic Quality Management (SQM) is a holistic approach that integrates quality principles into an organization's strategic planning and execution. It aligns quality goals with strategic objectives, fosters a customer-centric culture, and encourages data-driven decision-making. By implementing SQM effectively, organizations can achieve sustained quality excellence, enhance customer satisfaction, and gain a competitive advantage in the market.

E. Quality Culture and Leadership

Quality Culture and Leadership play a pivotal role in an organization's pursuit of excellence in quality management. A strong quality culture is the foundation upon which effective quality management practices are built, while leadership sets the tone, provides direction, and champions quality initiatives. In this section, we will delve into the in-depth understanding of Quality Culture and Leadership, their significance, and their interplay in fostering a culture of quality excellence.

Quality Culture:

Definition: Quality Culture refers to the collective mindset, values, beliefs, behaviors, and practices that an organization's members share with regard to quality. It represents the organization's commitment to quality as an integral part of its identity and daily operations.

Key Characteristics of a Quality Culture:

1. **Customer Focus:** A quality culture places customers at the center of its activities, constantly seeking to meet and exceed their expectations.

2. **Continuous Improvement:** Organizations with a strong quality culture are committed to ongoing improvement in all aspects of their operations.

3. **Employee Engagement:** Employees in a quality culture are actively engaged in quality initiatives, encouraged to provide feedback, and empowered to make decisions that impact quality.

4. **Leadership Commitment:** Leaders within the organization demonstrate a deep commitment to quality through their words and actions, setting an example for others.

5. **Transparency:** A culture of quality promotes open communication, transparency, and accountability at all levels.

6. **Problem-Solving Orientation:** Members of a quality culture are skilled in problem-solving and root cause analysis, addressing issues systematically.

7. **Data-Driven Decision-Making:** Quality decisions are based on data and evidence, rather than assumptions or intuition.

Significance of a Quality Culture:

- **Enhanced Quality:** A quality culture leads to consistently high-quality products or services, increasing customer satisfaction and loyalty.

- **Efficiency and Productivity:** Quality-driven practices improve efficiency and reduce waste, leading to cost savings.

- **Innovation:** Employees in a quality culture are more likely to suggest and implement innovative solutions to improve processes and products.

- **Risk Reduction:** A culture of quality is proactive in identifying and mitigating risks, preventing costly defects and errors.

- **Competitive Advantage:** Organizations with a strong quality culture often gain a competitive edge in the market.

Leadership in Quality:

Definition: Leadership in Quality refers to the role of top management and leaders in setting the quality agenda, providing direction, and fostering a culture of quality within the organization.

Key Aspects of Leadership in Quality:

1. **Commitment:** Leaders must demonstrate a strong commitment to quality, not only in words but through consistent actions and decisions.

2. **Vision:** Effective leaders communicate a clear vision for quality, setting the strategic direction for the organization.

3. **Resource Allocation:** Leaders ensure that the necessary resources, including personnel, budget, and technology, are allocated to support quality initiatives.

4. **Empowerment:** Leaders empower employees to take ownership of quality and make decisions that impact quality outcomes.

5. **Accountability:** Leaders hold themselves and their teams accountable for quality performance and outcomes.

6. **Training and Development:** Leaders invest in the training and development of employees to build their quality-related skills and capabilities.

Leadership Styles in Quality:

- **Transformational Leadership:** Transformational leaders inspire and motivate employees to achieve quality excellence by fostering a shared vision and a sense of purpose.

- **Servant Leadership:** Servant leaders prioritize the needs of their employees, providing support and resources to help them excel in their quality-related roles.

- **Democratic Leadership:** Democratic leaders involve employees in quality-related decision-making, leveraging their knowledge and expertise.

- **Lead by Example:** Leading by example involves leaders modeling the behaviors and attitudes they expect from others, including a commitment to quality.

Benefits of Leadership in Quality:

- **Cultural Influence:** Leaders shape the organization's culture, setting the tone for quality values and practices.

- **Direction and Focus:** Leadership provides direction and focus, ensuring that quality initiatives are aligned with strategic objectives.

- **Resource Mobilization:** Leaders allocate resources strategically to support quality improvement efforts.

- **Employee Engagement:** Effective leadership engages employees in quality initiatives, fostering a sense of ownership and accountability.

- **Decision-Making:** Quality-oriented leaders make informed, data-driven decisions that benefit quality outcomes.

Challenges in Fostering a Quality Culture and Leadership:

1. **Cultural Change:** Shifting to a culture of quality may face resistance from entrenched cultural norms and practices.

2. **Resource Constraints:** Investing in leadership development and cultural change efforts can require significant resources.

3. **Sustainability:** Maintaining a strong quality culture and leadership commitment over time can be challenging.

4. **Measuring Impact:** It can be difficult to quantify the direct impact of quality culture and leadership on organizational performance.

In conclusion, Quality Culture and Leadership are integral components of successful quality management. A strong quality culture shapes the organization's identity and daily operations, while effective leadership sets the tone and direction for quality initiatives. Together, they foster an environment where quality becomes an intrinsic part of the organization's DNA, leading to consistently high-quality products or services and sustained excellence.

CHAPTER 4

Quality Assurance Practices

Quality Assurance Practices are the bedrock of ensuring that products and services consistently meet or exceed customer expectations. In today's competitive business landscape, organizations across various industries rely on robust quality assurance processes to not only prevent defects and errors but also to instill confidence in customers, regulatory bodies, and stakeholders. This section will delve into the world of Quality Assurance Practices, exploring their purpose, methodologies, and the critical role they play in delivering uncompromising quality.

A. Quality Assurance vs. Quality Control

Quality Assurance (QA) and Quality Control (QC) are two essential components of an organization's approach to ensuring product and service quality. While these terms are sometimes used interchangeably, they represent distinct yet complementary aspects of the broader field of quality management. In this section, we will delve into the in-depth understanding of Quality Assurance and Quality Control, their differences, similarities, and their roles in maintaining and improving quality.

Quality Assurance (QA):

Definition: Quality Assurance (QA) refers to the systematic and proactive approach taken by organizations to prevent defects, errors, and deviations in processes, products, or services. It encompasses the processes, standards, and guidelines that ensure that quality requirements are met throughout the entire product or service lifecycle.

Key Aspects of Quality Assurance:

1. **Process-Oriented:** QA focuses on the processes used to create products or deliver services. It aims to establish and maintain well-defined, standardized processes that consistently produce high-quality outcomes.

2. **Preventive:** QA is primarily preventive in nature, with the goal of identifying and addressing potential issues before they result in defects or nonconformities.

3. **Standards and Guidelines:** QA relies on established standards, best practices, and quality management systems to guide and govern processes. ISO 9001 is a well-known standard for QA.

4. **Documentation:** QA emphasizes thorough documentation of processes and procedures to ensure consistency, traceability, and compliance.

5. **Training and Competence:** It involves training and developing employees to ensure that they are competent in their roles and capable of adhering to established quality standards.

6. **Continuous Improvement:** QA fosters a culture of continuous improvement, with regular reviews and adjustments to processes to enhance quality and efficiency.

Benefits of Quality Assurance:

- **Prevention of Defects:** QA prevents defects from occurring in the first place, reducing the need for corrective actions and minimizing waste.

- **Consistency:** Standardized processes and procedures lead to consistent, reliable outcomes.

- **Cost Savings:** By preventing defects and errors, QA reduces the cost of rework, scrap, and customer complaints.

- **Customer Satisfaction:** High-quality products or services resulting from QA practices enhance customer satisfaction and loyalty.

Quality Control (QC):

Definition: Quality Control (QC) is the systematic process of evaluating and verifying that products or services meet established quality standards and specifications. It involves inspecting, testing, and measuring products or services to identify defects or nonconformities and taking corrective actions when necessary.

Key Aspects of Quality Control:

1. **Product-Oriented:** QC focuses on the final product or service, with the objective of identifying and correcting deviations from established quality standards.

2. **Detective:** QC is primarily detective in nature, aiming to identify defects or issues after they have occurred but before they reach the customer.

3. **Sampling and Inspection:** QC often involves sampling techniques and inspections to assess product or service quality. Control charts, statistical analysis, and inspections are common QC tools.

4. **Corrective Actions:** When defects or nonconformities are identified, QC initiates corrective actions to address the issues and bring the product or service into compliance.

5. **Customer-Focused:** QC ensures that products or services meet customer requirements and specifications.

Benefits of Quality Control:

- **Defect Detection:** QC helps identify defects and

nonconformities, preventing subpar products or services from reaching the customer.

- **Compliance:** It ensures that products or services adhere to established quality standards and specifications.

- **Data for Improvement:** QC data provides valuable insights for process improvement and corrective action planning.

- **Customer Confidence:** Effective QC practices instill confidence in customers, demonstrating an organization's commitment to quality.

Comparative Analysis:

1. **Timing:**

   - **QA:** QA activities occur throughout the entire product or service lifecycle, focusing on prevention.

   - **QC:** QC activities occur during or after the production or service delivery phase, focusing on detection.

2. **Nature:**

   - **QA:** QA is preventive and process-oriented, aiming to establish and maintain processes that consistently produce quality outcomes.

   - **QC:** QC is detective and product-oriented, focusing on

evaluating the final product or service for compliance with standards.

3. **Role:**

- **QA:** QA ensures that the right processes are in place to prevent defects and errors.

- **QC:** QC verifies that the product or service produced conforms to established standards.

4. **Approach:**

- **QA:** QA relies on process improvement, standardization, and documentation.

- **QC:** QC uses inspection, testing, and measurement to assess product or service quality.

5. **Focus:**

- **QA:** QA focuses on avoiding quality problems before they occur.

- **QC:** QC focuses on identifying and correcting quality problems after they occur but before they reach the customer.

In summary, Quality Assurance (QA) and Quality Control (QC) are complementary approaches to quality management. QA is a proactive, preventive approach focused on processes, standards, and preventing defects, while QC is a reactive, detective approach focused on evaluating the final product or service for compliance with established standards. Both QA and QC are crucial in ensuring that products or services meet quality requirements and customer expectations.

B. Quality Auditing

Quality Auditing is a systematic and objective examination of an organization's quality management system (QMS) and processes to ensure compliance with established standards, regulations, and best practices. Auditing is a critical component of Quality Assurance, providing an independent and comprehensive assessment of an organization's adherence to quality standards and the effectiveness of its quality control measures. In this section, we will delve into the in-depth understanding of Quality Auditing, its types, methodologies, and the significant role it plays in maintaining and enhancing product and service quality.

Purpose of Quality Auditing:

1. **Compliance Verification:** Auditing ensures that an organization complies with relevant quality standards, regulations, and industry-specific requirements.

2. **Process Evaluation:** Auditors assess the effectiveness of an

organization's quality management processes, identifying areas for improvement.

3. **Risk Mitigation:** Auditing helps identify and address potential risks and vulnerabilities that could impact product or service quality.

4. **Continuous Improvement:** Auditing provides valuable feedback for process optimization and ongoing quality improvement efforts.

5. **Objective Assessment:** Auditors provide an independent and objective evaluation of an organization's quality practices, offering an unbiased perspective.

Types of Quality Audits:

1. **Internal Audits:** Internal audits are conducted by personnel within the organization to assess its internal processes, procedures, and adherence to quality standards and regulations. These audits help identify areas for improvement and ensure internal compliance.

2. **External Audits:** External audits are conducted by independent third-party organizations or regulatory bodies to verify an organization's compliance with external standards and regulations. Examples include ISO certification audits and regulatory compliance audits.

3. **Supplier Audits:** Organizations may audit their suppliers to ensure that purchased products or services meet quality requirements. Supplier audits are essential to maintain product quality in the supply chain.

Key Steps in the Quality Auditing Process:

1. **Audit Planning:** Define the audit objectives, scope, and criteria. Develop an audit plan that outlines the audit schedule, team, and resources required.

2. **Audit Preparation:** Review relevant documentation, standards, and regulations. Notify the auditee (the organization being audited) of the upcoming audit and request necessary documents and access.

3. **On-Site Audit:** Conduct the audit, which includes interviews, document reviews, process observations, and data collection. Auditors evaluate the organization's processes, controls, and compliance.

4. **Audit Findings:** Compile and document audit findings, including nonconformities (instances of non-compliance), observations, and opportunities for improvement.

5. **Report Generation:** Prepare an audit report that outlines the audit's objectives, scope, findings, and recommendations. The report is typically shared with the auditee for their response.

6. **Corrective Actions:** The auditee responds to the audit findings by developing and implementing corrective actions to address nonconformities and improve processes.

7. **Follow-Up Audit:** In some cases, a follow-up audit is conducted to verify the effectiveness of corrective actions and ensure that identified issues have been resolved.

Auditor Qualifications:

Auditors should possess specific qualifications and competencies, including:

- **Knowledge of Quality Standards:** Auditors must be well-versed in relevant quality standards, regulations, and industry-specific requirements.

- **Audit Training:** Proper training in audit methodologies, techniques, and best practices is essential.

- **Communication Skills:** Effective communication is crucial for conducting interviews, documenting findings, and reporting results.

- **Analytical Skills:** Auditors should have strong analytical skills to evaluate processes, identify nonconformities, and make recommendations.

- **Independence and Objectivity:** Auditors must maintain

independence and objectivity to provide unbiased assessments.

Benefits of Quality Auditing:

1. **Assurance of Quality:** Auditing provides assurance that an organization's products or services meet quality standards and regulations.

2. **Risk Identification:** Auditors identify potential risks and vulnerabilities that could impact product quality or compliance.

3. **Process Improvement:** Auditing uncovers opportunities for process improvement and optimization.

4. **Compliance:** Audits ensure that the organization complies with relevant quality standards and regulations.

5. **Customer Confidence:** Successful audits enhance customer confidence in the organization's ability to deliver high-quality products or services.

Challenges in Quality Auditing:

1. **Resource Intensive:** Auditing can be resource-intensive in terms of time, personnel, and costs.

2. **Resistance:** Auditees may resist audits due to concerns about negative findings or disruption to their processes.

3. **Complexity:** Auditing complex processes or industries may require specialized knowledge and expertise.

In conclusion, Quality Auditing is a critical component of Quality Assurance, providing an independent and objective assessment of an organization's adherence to quality standards and regulations. It serves as a proactive means to identify nonconformities, improve processes, and assure customers and stakeholders of product and service quality. By conducting thorough and effective audits, organizations can enhance their quality management systems and maintain a competitive edge in the market.

C. Process Documentation and Standardization

Process Documentation and Standardization are foundational elements of Quality Assurance (QA) that help organizations establish consistent and repeatable processes, ensuring that products or services meet defined quality standards and customer expectations. In this section, we will explore in-depth the concepts of Process Documentation and Standardization, their significance, methodologies, and their pivotal role in achieving and maintaining high-quality outcomes.

Process Documentation:

Definition: Process Documentation involves the systematic and comprehensive recording of an organization's processes, procedures, workflows, and activities. This documentation provides a clear and structured representation of how tasks are performed, ensuring transparency and accountability.

Key Aspects of Process Documentation:

1. **Clarity:** Process documentation aims to make processes clear and understandable, ensuring that employees can follow them accurately.

2. **Standardization:** It establishes a consistent framework for executing tasks, reducing variability and increasing reliability.

3. **Transparency:** Well-documented processes promote transparency, allowing stakeholders to understand how work is done.

4. **Compliance:** Process documentation often aligns with quality standards and regulatory requirements, helping organizations meet compliance obligations.

5. **Continuous Improvement:** It serves as a foundation for process analysis and optimization, identifying areas for improvement.

Methodologies for Process Documentation:

1. **Flowcharts:** Flowcharts use symbols and shapes to visually represent the sequence of steps and decision points in a process.

2. **Process Maps:** Process maps provide a detailed overview of a process, including inputs, outputs, activities, and responsibilities.

3. **Standard Operating Procedures (SOPs):** SOPs are comprehensive written documents that outline step-by-step instructions for performing specific tasks or processes.

4. **Checklists:** Checklists are simple tools that list essential steps or tasks to ensure completeness and accuracy in process execution.

5. **Narrative Descriptions:** Narrative descriptions provide written explanations of processes, offering a detailed account of each step.

Process Standardization:

Definition: Process Standardization involves the establishment of uniform and consistent procedures and practices across an organization. Standardization ensures that processes are executed in the same way every time, reducing variability and enhancing predictability.

Key Aspects of Process Standardization:

1. **Consistency:** Standardized processes eliminate variations in how tasks are performed, leading to consistent outcomes.

2. **Quality Control:** Standardization allows organizations to implement quality control measures effectively.

3. **Efficiency:** Standardized processes often lead to improved efficiency, as employees become familiar with a consistent set of procedures.

4. **Reduced Errors:** Standardized processes reduce the likelihood of errors and defects due to clear guidelines and best practices.

5. **Training and Onboarding:** Standardized processes facilitate employee training and onboarding by providing a structured framework.

Methodologies for Process Standardization:

1. **Documented Procedures:** Create detailed written procedures and guidelines for each step in a process.

2. **Training and Education:** Ensure that employees are trained on standardized processes and understand their role in execution.

3. **Quality Management Systems (QMS):** Implement QMS

software and tools to automate and standardize processes.

4. **Performance Metrics:** Develop Key Performance Indicators (KPIs) to measure process performance and compliance with standards.

Benefits of Process Documentation and Standardization:

1. **Consistency:** Standardized processes ensure that tasks are performed consistently, reducing variability and improving predictability.

2. **Quality Assurance:** Documentation and standardization help organizations adhere to quality standards and meet regulatory requirements.

3. **Efficiency:** Standardized processes often lead to increased efficiency and reduced cycle times.

4. **Training and Onboarding:** Well-documented processes simplify training and onboarding processes for new employees.

5. **Process Improvement:** Process documentation provides a baseline for process analysis and optimization, enabling continuous improvement efforts.

6. **Risk Mitigation:** Standardized processes help identify and mitigate risks more effectively.

Challenges in Process Documentation and Standardization:

1. **Resistance to Change:** Employees may resist the adoption of standardized processes if they perceive them as disruptive.

2. **Resource Intensive:** The process of documenting and standardizing procedures can be resource-intensive.

3. **Maintaining Relevance:** Processes must be regularly reviewed and updated to remain relevant and effective.

In conclusion, Process Documentation and Standardization are essential components of Quality Assurance that enable organizations to achieve and maintain high-quality outcomes. Through clear and comprehensive documentation of processes and the establishment of consistent practices, organizations can reduce variability, improve efficiency, meet compliance requirements, and foster a culture of continuous improvement. These practices are fundamental to ensuring that products or services consistently meet quality standards and customer expectations.

D. Supplier Quality Management

Supplier Quality Management (SQM) is a critical aspect of Quality Assurance that focuses on ensuring that the products, components, or services provided by suppliers meet the required quality standards and specifications. In today's globalized and interconnected business landscape, organizations rely on a network of suppliers and partners to deliver goods and services. Effective SQM is essential to maintain product quality, mitigate risks, and uphold the organization's reputation. In this section, we will delve into the in-depth understanding of Supplier Quality Management, its significance, methodologies, and its pivotal role in maintaining and enhancing product and service quality.

Significance of Supplier Quality Management:

1. **Risk Mitigation:** Effective SQM helps identify and mitigate potential risks associated with supplier products or services, reducing the likelihood of defects or disruptions in the supply chain.

2. **Consistency:** SQM ensures that supplier-provided materials or services consistently meet quality standards, reducing variability in the manufacturing or service delivery process.

3. **Cost Reduction:** By minimizing defects and nonconformities from suppliers, SQM reduces the cost of rework, scrap, and warranty claims.

4. **Customer Satisfaction:** High-quality products or services, resulting from SQM, enhance customer satisfaction and loyalty.

5. **Regulatory Compliance:** SQM helps organizations comply with regulatory requirements, especially in industries with strict quality and safety regulations.

Key Components of Supplier Quality Management:

1. **Supplier Evaluation and Selection:** Organizations must assess potential suppliers based on criteria such as quality, reliability, financial stability, and ethical practices before entering into agreements.

2. **Supplier Audits:** Conduct regular audits of supplier facilities to ensure compliance with quality standards and contractual obligations.

3. **Supplier Performance Metrics:** Establish Key Performance Indicators (KPIs) to measure supplier performance in areas such as on-time delivery, defect rates, and responsiveness.

4. **Supplier Collaboration:** Collaborate with suppliers to improve processes, share best practices, and address quality issues collectively.

5. **Supplier Training and Support:** Provide necessary training and support to help suppliers meet quality standards and requirements.

6. **Supplier Development:** Work with suppliers to develop their capabilities and quality management systems.

Key Methodologies and Practices in Supplier Quality Management:

1. **Supplier Audits:** Conduct regular supplier audits to assess compliance with quality standards, evaluate manufacturing processes, and identify areas for improvement.

2. **Supplier Corrective Action Requests (SCARs):** When quality issues arise, issue SCARs to suppliers, detailing the nonconformance and requesting corrective actions.

3. **Supplier Scorecards:** Implement supplier scorecards to track and compare supplier performance over time, making it easier to identify top-performing and underperforming suppliers.

4. **Supplier Relationship Management (SRM):** Develop strong relationships with key suppliers through SRM programs, fostering collaboration and mutual improvement.

5. **Risk Assessment:** Continuously assess supplier risks, including geopolitical, financial, and quality-related risks, and develop risk mitigation strategies.

Challenges in Supplier Quality Management:

1. **Globalization:** Managing suppliers from different regions with varying regulatory environments and cultural norms can be challenging.

2. **Communication Barriers:** Language barriers and differences in communication styles can hinder effective collaboration with international suppliers.

3. **Supply Chain Complexity:** As supply chains become more complex, it becomes increasingly difficult to monitor and manage every supplier effectively.

4. **Resource Intensive:** Implementing robust SQM processes and conducting supplier audits can be resource-intensive.

5. **Supplier Resistance:** Suppliers may resist sharing sensitive information or making necessary changes to their processes.

Best Practices in Supplier Quality Management:

1. **Clear Quality Agreements:** Establish clear quality agreements with suppliers, specifying quality standards, performance expectations, and responsibilities.

2. **Regular Performance Reviews:** Conduct regular performance reviews with suppliers to discuss KPIs, quality issues, and improvement plans.

3. **Continuous Improvement:** Encourage suppliers to pursue continuous improvement initiatives and share best practices.

4. **Supplier Collaboration:** Develop collaborative relationships with key suppliers, involving them in problem-solving and

innovation efforts.

5. **Technology Integration:** Leverage technology, such as Supplier Relationship Management (SRM) software, to streamline communication, data sharing, and performance tracking.

In conclusion, Supplier Quality Management is a critical aspect of Quality Assurance that ensures that supplier-provided products or services meet the required quality standards and specifications. Effective SQM is essential for mitigating risks, reducing costs, maintaining consistency, and enhancing customer satisfaction. By implementing robust SQM practices and fostering collaborative relationships with suppliers, organizations can strengthen their supply chain, protect their brand reputation, and deliver high-quality products or services to customers.

E. Continuous Improvement in Quality Assurance

Continuous Improvement in Quality Assurance (QA) is a systematic and ongoing effort to enhance the quality of products, services, and processes. It is a fundamental principle of quality management, emphasizing the need to continually assess and refine QA practices. Continuous improvement fosters innovation, efficiency, and competitiveness, ensuring that organizations can meet and exceed customer expectations. In this section, we will delve into the in-depth understanding of Continuous Improvement in QA, its methodologies, tools, and the critical role it plays in achieving and maintaining high-quality outcomes.

Key Concepts in Continuous Improvement:

1. **PDCA Cycle:** The Plan-Do-Check-Act (PDCA) cycle, also known as the Deming Cycle, is a fundamental framework for continuous improvement. It involves planning a change (Plan), implementing it (Do), assessing the results (Check), and taking corrective actions (Act) to further improve.

2. **Kaizen:** Kaizen is a Japanese term that means "change for better" or "continuous improvement." It emphasizes small, incremental improvements made by everyone in the organization on a daily basis.

3. **Lean Principles:** Lean principles focus on eliminating waste and optimizing processes. Key concepts include value stream mapping, 5S (Sort, Set in order, Shine, Standardize, Sustain), and Just-in-Time (JIT) production.

4. **Six Sigma:** Six Sigma is a data-driven methodology that aims to reduce defects and variation in processes. It utilizes statistical tools and techniques to identify and address root causes of quality issues.

Continuous Improvement Methodologies:

1. **Kaizen Events:** Kaizen events, also known as Rapid Improvement Events, are short-term, focused efforts to address specific problems or improve processes. They involve cross-functional teams and aim for quick, tangible results.

2. **DMAIC:** DMAIC (Define, Measure, Analyze, Improve, Control) is a structured approach used in Six Sigma projects. It guides teams through the phases of problem-solving and process improvement.

3. **5 Whys Analysis:** The 5 Whys is a simple yet powerful technique for identifying the root cause of a problem by asking "Why?" repeatedly until the root cause is uncovered.

4. **Root Cause Analysis (RCA):** RCA is a systematic process for identifying the underlying causes of problems or defects. Techniques such as Fishbone diagrams (Ishikawa diagrams) and Fault Tree Analysis are often used.

5. **Pareto Analysis:** Pareto Analysis helps prioritize improvement efforts by focusing on the most significant factors contributing to a problem. The 80/20 rule (80% of effects come from 20% of causes) is often applied.

Steps in Continuous Improvement:

1. **Identification of Opportunities:** Identify areas or processes

that require improvement through data analysis, customer feedback, or performance metrics.

2. **Problem Definition:** Clearly define the problem or opportunity for improvement, setting specific goals and objectives.

3. **Data Collection and Analysis:** Gather relevant data to understand the current state of the process and identify root causes of issues.

4. **Solution Generation:** Brainstorm and evaluate potential solutions or changes to address the identified problems.

5. **Implementation:** Implement the selected solution or changes, carefully monitoring the process during this phase.

6. **Measurement and Evaluation:** Continuously monitor and measure the impact of the changes to ensure they are achieving the desired results.

7. **Standardization:** Once successful improvements are identified, standardize the new processes or practices across the organization.

8. **Documentation:** Document the entire improvement process, including data, actions, and results, for future reference and knowledge sharing.

Benefits of Continuous Improvement in QA:

1. **Quality Enhancement:** Continuous improvement leads to higher product and service quality, resulting in increased customer satisfaction.

2. **Efficiency:** Streamlined processes and reduced waste lead to improved efficiency and cost savings.

3. **Competitiveness:** Organizations that embrace continuous improvement can respond more effectively to changing market conditions and maintain a competitive edge.

4. **Employee Engagement:** Involving employees in continuous improvement initiatives fosters a culture of engagement, empowerment, and innovation.

5. **Risk Mitigation:** Addressing issues proactively through continuous improvement helps prevent larger quality problems or disruptions.

Challenges in Continuous Improvement:

1. **Resistance to Change:** Employees may resist change, especially if they perceive it as disruptive to their routines or roles.

2. **Resource Constraints:** Implementing continuous improvement initiatives may require additional resources,

such as time, personnel, and technology.

3. **Lack of Data and Metrics:** Insufficient data or the absence of appropriate metrics can hinder effective analysis and improvement efforts.

4. **Lack of Leadership Support:** Without strong leadership support and commitment to continuous improvement, initiatives may falter.

In conclusion, Continuous Improvement in Quality Assurance is a dynamic and proactive approach to enhancing quality, efficiency, and competitiveness. By systematically identifying, analyzing, and addressing issues or opportunities for improvement, organizations can deliver higher-quality products and services, meet customer expectations, and thrive in today's ever-evolving business environment. Continuous improvement methodologies and tools empower organizations to adapt, innovate, and excel in their pursuit of excellence.

CHAPTER 5

Quality Control and Inspection

Quality Control and Inspection are pivotal components of ensuring that products and services meet the defined quality standards and specifications. They serve as the final gatekeepers in the quality assurance process, focusing on the systematic examination, measurement, and verification of products, components, or services to identify any deviations from the established quality criteria. In this section, we will explore in-depth the concepts of Quality Control and Inspection, their methodologies, tools, and the critical role they play in maintaining and delivering high-quality outcomes to customers and stakeholders.

A. Statistical Process Control (SPC)

Statistical Process Control (SPC) is a powerful methodology used in quality control to monitor, control, and improve processes. SPC utilizes statistical techniques to analyze data and assess the stability and performance of a process, ultimately ensuring that it operates within defined quality parameters. This section provides an in-depth exploration of SPC, its principles, methods, and its critical role in maintaining and enhancing product or service quality.

Key Principles of Statistical Process Control:

1. **Variation is Inevitable:** SPC recognizes that there will always be natural variation in any process. Understanding and distinguishing between common cause (natural) and special cause (assignable) variation is essential.

2. **Data-Driven Decision Making:** SPC relies on data and statistical analysis to make informed decisions about process stability, capability, and improvement.

3. **Process Control:** The primary goal of SPC is to keep processes in control, meaning they operate consistently within defined limits and exhibit predictable variation.

4. **Continuous Improvement:** SPC is closely tied to the concept of continuous improvement, with the aim of reducing process variability and enhancing overall quality.

Key Components of Statistical Process Control:

1. **Data Collection:** SPC begins with the collection of data related to the process. Data can be collected in various forms, such as measurements, counts, or observations.

2. **Control Charts:** Control charts, also known as Shewhart

charts or process-behavior charts, are the central tool in SPC. They visually display data points over time, allowing practitioners to identify trends, patterns, and anomalies.

3. **Common Cause Variation:** This refers to natural variation inherent in a process. It is represented by data points within the control limits on a control chart.

4. **Special Cause Variation:** Special cause variation is attributed to specific factors or events that disrupt the normal operation of a process. It is indicated by data points outside the control limits or other unusual patterns on a control chart.

5. **Control Limits:** Control limits are the upper and lower bounds on a control chart that define the range of expected variation for a stable process.

6. **Process Capability Analysis:** Process capability measures, such as Cp, Cpk, Pp, and Ppk, assess the ability of a process to consistently produce products or services that meet specified requirements.

Steps in Implementing Statistical Process Control:

1. **Define the Process:** Clearly define the process to be controlled and identify the key parameters and quality characteristics.

2. **Data Collection:** Collect data over time, ensuring that it

accurately represents the process. Common data collection methods include sampling and measurement.

3. **Select Control Charts:** Choose the appropriate control chart based on the type of data and the quality characteristic being monitored.

4. **Establish Control Limits:** Calculate control limits based on historical data or process specifications. Control limits should encompass the expected variation of the process.

5. **Plot Data:** Plot the collected data on the control chart, marking data points over time.

6. **Monitor and Interpret:** Continuously monitor the control chart to detect trends, shifts, or patterns that indicate special cause variation.

7. **Investigate and Take Action:** When special cause variation is identified, investigate the root cause and take corrective actions to address the issue.

8. **Review and Improve:** Periodically review the control chart and process performance to assess the effectiveness of corrective actions and identify opportunities for process improvement.

Benefits of Statistical Process Control:

1. **Early Defect Detection:** SPC helps identify quality issues in real-time, allowing for prompt corrective action and preventing the production of defective products or services.

2. **Improved Process Stability:** By maintaining processes within control limits, SPC enhances process stability and consistency.

3. **Efficiency:** SPC reduces waste, rework, and production costs by minimizing variability and defects.

4. **Data-Driven Decision Making:** SPC provides data and insights that guide informed decision-making, process optimization, and continuous improvement.

5. **Enhanced Productivity:** SPC allows organizations to allocate resources efficiently and focus on value-added activities.

Challenges in Statistical Process Control:

1. **Data Quality:** SPC relies on accurate and representative data. Poor data quality can lead to incorrect conclusions and ineffective control.

2. **Resistance to Change:** Employees may resist SPC implementation, especially if they perceive it as additional work or scrutiny.

3. **Complexity:** SPC can be complex, requiring statistical expertise and tools for effective implementation.

4. **Integration with Processes:** Integrating SPC into existing processes and workflows can be challenging, requiring careful planning and training.

In conclusion, Statistical Process Control is a robust methodology for monitoring, controlling, and improving processes to achieve and maintain high-quality outcomes. By using control charts and data-driven decision-making, organizations can proactively detect and address issues, reduce variability, and enhance overall process performance. SPC plays a pivotal role in quality management, ensuring that products or services consistently meet or exceed customer expectations while facilitating a culture of continuous improvement within organizations.

B. Control Charts and Process Variation

Control charts are fundamental tools in Statistical Process Control (SPC) that enable organizations to monitor and manage process variation systematically. They provide a visual representation of process data over time, helping practitioners distinguish between common cause and special cause variation. This section explores control charts, their types, construction, interpretation, and their vital role in maintaining and enhancing product or service quality.

Types of Control Charts:

1. **Variable Control Charts:** These control charts are used when the data being monitored are measurements, such as dimensions, weights, or temperatures. Common variable control charts include X-bar and R charts, X-bar and S charts, and individual/moving range (I-MR) charts.

2. **Attribute Control Charts:** Attribute control charts are employed when data are in the form of counts or proportions, such as the number of defects, conforming units, or nonconforming units. Common attribute control charts include p-charts, np-charts, c-charts, and u-charts.

Key Elements of Control Charts:

1. **Data Points:** Data points represent measurements or counts collected at regular intervals from the process being monitored.

2. **Central Line (CL):** The central line on a control chart represents the process's historical average or expected value.

3. **Control Limits (UCL and LCL):** Upper Control Limits (UCL) and Lower Control Limits (LCL) are calculated based on the historical process data and represent the expected range of variation for a stable process.

4. **Data Points on the Chart:** Data points are plotted on the control chart over time, helping visualize the process's performance.

Interpreting Control Charts:

1. **In-Control Process:** If all data points fall within the control limits and there are no discernible patterns or trends, the process is considered in control. Any variation observed is due to common causes, which are inherent to the process.

2. **Out-of-Control Process:** If data points exceed the control limits, display patterns, or exhibit trends, the process is considered out of control. Special cause variation, often attributed to specific events or factors, may be present and requires investigation and corrective action.

Control Chart Patterns:

1. **Trends:** Trends involve consecutive data points consistently increasing or decreasing over time, suggesting a shift in the process.

2. **Cycles:** Cycles indicate repeating patterns in the data, which may be related to seasonal or periodic factors affecting the process.

3. **Shifts:** Shifts are abrupt changes in the process mean or level, often resulting from specific events or process adjustments.

4. **Assignable Causes:** Special cause variation, also known as assignable causes, includes factors or events that are not part of the normal process and lead to non-random patterns on the control chart.

Steps in Using Control Charts:

1. **Collect Data:** Gather data points at regular intervals from the process.

2. **Determine Control Limits:** Calculate control limits based on the data, typically using statistical formulas such as standard deviation.

3. **Plot Data Points:** Create the control chart by plotting the collected data points over time.

4. **Analyze the Chart:** Examine the control chart for patterns, trends, or data points outside the control limits.

5. **Identify Special Causes:** When special cause variation is identified, investigate the root cause and take corrective action to address it.

6. **Continuous Monitoring:** Continue monitoring the process and reviewing the control chart to ensure stability and make ongoing improvements.

Benefits of Control Charts and Process Variation Analysis:

1. **Early Problem Detection:** Control charts enable the early detection of process issues, allowing for timely corrective actions to prevent defects or deviations.

2. **Data-Driven Decision Making:** Control charts provide data-driven insights into process performance, guiding decisions on process adjustments and improvements.

3. **Process Optimization:** By identifying and addressing sources of variation, control charts help organizations optimize their processes for consistency and quality.

4. **Cost Reduction:** Reduced process variation leads to cost savings by minimizing waste, rework, and defects.

5. **Continuous Improvement:** Control charts are integral to the concept of continuous improvement, driving organizations to enhance their processes continually.

Challenges in Control Chart Implementation:

1. **Data Quality:** Control charts rely on accurate and representative data. Poor data quality can lead to incorrect conclusions.

2. **Resistance to Change:** Employees may resist control chart implementation if they perceive it as additional work or

scrutiny.

3. **Complexity:** Control charts can be complex, requiring statistical expertise for effective implementation and interpretation.

4. **Integration with Processes:** Integrating control chart usage into existing processes and workflows can be challenging, requiring careful planning and training.

In conclusion, control charts and the analysis of process variation are indispensable tools in ensuring process stability and enhancing product or service quality. By visually representing process data and distinguishing between common and special cause variation, organizations can proactively manage and improve their processes, minimize defects, and meet or exceed customer expectations consistently. Control charts play a pivotal role in quality management, fostering a culture of data-driven decision-making and continuous improvement within organizations.

C. Sampling Techniques and Inspection

Sampling techniques and inspection methods are essential components of quality control, allowing organizations to assess the quality of products or services efficiently without examining every single unit. This section delves into the in-depth understanding of various sampling techniques, inspection methods, their applications, advantages, and challenges in ensuring and maintaining high-quality outcomes.

Importance of Sampling and Inspection:

1. **Efficiency:** Sampling reduces the time and resources required to inspect every item in a large production batch, making quality control more cost-effective.

2. **Risk Mitigation:** Inspection helps identify and remove defective items from the supply chain, reducing the risk of delivering subpar products to customers.

3. **Compliance:** Inspection ensures that products meet regulatory requirements and adhere to quality standards.

4. **Data for Decision Making:** Inspection data provides valuable insights for decision-making, process improvement, and supplier feedback.

Sampling Techniques:

1. **Random Sampling:** In random sampling, items are selected entirely by chance, giving each item in the population an equal probability of being chosen. This method is unbiased but may not detect localized issues.

2. **Stratified Sampling:** Stratified sampling divides the

population into subgroups or strata based on certain characteristics. Samples are then randomly selected from each stratum. This method is useful when there are known variations within the population.

3. **Systematic Sampling:** Systematic sampling involves selecting items at regular intervals from a list or production line. It provides a balance between randomness and efficiency but can be sensitive to patterns.

4. **Cluster Sampling:** Cluster sampling divides the population into clusters, then selects entire clusters at random. It is useful when clusters represent naturally occurring groups.

Inspection Methods:

1. **100% Inspection:** In this method, every item in a batch is inspected thoroughly. It is time-consuming and expensive but ensures that no defective items pass inspection.

2. **Acceptance Sampling:** Acceptance sampling involves inspecting a random sample of items from a batch. The decision to accept or reject the entire batch is based on the sample's quality.

3. **Variable Inspection:** Variable inspection measures specific characteristics, such as dimensions or weight, and compares them to predefined tolerances or specifications.

4. **Attribute Inspection:** Attribute inspection classifies items as conforming or nonconforming based on specific criteria, such as the presence of defects.

Common Acceptance Sampling Plans:

1. **Single Sampling Plan:** A single sample is taken, and the entire batch is accepted or rejected based on the sample's quality.

2. **Double Sampling Plan:** If the first sample's results are inconclusive, a second sample is taken. The decision to accept or reject depends on the results of both samples.

3. **Multiple Sampling Plan:** Multiple samples are taken, and the decision to accept or reject is based on a predefined number of nonconforming items across all samples.

Advantages of Sampling and Inspection:

1. **Efficiency:** Sampling reduces inspection time and costs, making it feasible to assess large batches.

2. **Statistical Confidence:** Sampling can provide statistically valid insights into the quality of a population.

3. **Quick Decision-Making:** Sampling allows for rapid decisions regarding the acceptance or rejection of batches.

4. **Reduced Handling:** In many cases, sampling is less

disruptive to production processes than 100% inspection.

Challenges in Sampling and Inspection:

1. **Sampling Error:** Random sampling can introduce sampling error, which means the sample may not perfectly represent the entire population.

2. **Sampling Bias:** If sampling is not truly random or if certain factors influence the selection of items, sampling bias can occur.

3. **Small Batch Sizes:** In cases of small batch sizes, random sampling may not provide adequate coverage.

4. **Dynamic Processes:** Sampling may not be suitable for processes that change rapidly or have high variability.

In conclusion, sampling techniques and inspection methods are vital tools in quality control, enabling organizations to efficiently assess product or service quality, reduce costs, and mitigate risks. The choice of sampling method and inspection approach should be tailored to the specific context and objectives, considering factors such as batch size, production processes, and the desired level of confidence in the assessment. When implemented effectively, these techniques contribute to maintaining and enhancing the overall quality of products and services, leading to customer satisfaction and operational efficiency.

D. Root Cause Analysis

Root Cause Analysis (RCA) is a systematic and structured process for identifying the underlying reasons or causes of problems, defects, or issues within processes or systems. It is a critical component of quality control and quality assurance, as it aims to address the source of problems rather than merely treating symptoms. In this section, we will delve into the in-depth understanding of Root Cause Analysis, its methodologies, tools, and its pivotal role in preventing the recurrence of quality issues.

Key Concepts in Root Cause Analysis:

1. **Root Cause:** The root cause is the fundamental reason behind a problem or defect. Identifying the root cause is essential to prevent the issue from happening again.

2. **Symptom vs. Cause:** Symptoms are the visible or apparent indicators of a problem, while causes are the underlying factors that lead to those symptoms.

3. **System Thinking:** RCA often involves examining the entire system or process, as problems can result from interactions between various components.

4. **Preventive Action:** Once the root cause is identified, preventive actions can be taken to eliminate or mitigate the cause and prevent future occurrences of the problem.

Methodologies and Tools for Root Cause Analysis:

1. **Ishikawa Diagram (Fishbone Diagram):** This tool helps visualize potential causes of a problem by categorizing them into categories like People, Process, Equipment, Materials, and Environment (the 5 Whys technique can be applied within each category).

2. **5 Whys Analysis:** The 5 Whys technique involves asking "Why?" repeatedly to delve deeper into the causes of a problem, uncovering the root cause by addressing the issue's immediate and underlying causes.

3. **Fault Tree Analysis (FTA):** FTA is a systematic method used in engineering and safety analysis to identify the combinations of events or factors that can lead to a specific undesirable outcome.

4. **Pareto Analysis:** Pareto analysis focuses on identifying the most significant contributing factors to a problem. It follows the 80/20 rule, where 80% of the effects result from 20% of the causes.

5. **Cause-and-Effect Analysis:** Cause-and-effect diagrams, also known as fishbone or Ishikawa diagrams, visually represent the relationships between various factors and the problem they cause.

6. **Root Cause Analysis Teams:** Involving cross-functional teams with diverse expertise can help uncover a broader range of potential causes.

Steps in Root Cause Analysis:

1. **Problem Identification:** Clearly define the problem or issue and its impact on quality, safety, or performance.

2. **Data Collection:** Gather relevant data and information related to the problem, including when, where, and how it occurred.

3. **Idea Generation:** Brainstorm potential causes and factors contributing to the problem. Use tools like the Ishikawa diagram or 5 Whys.

4. **Cause Prioritization:** Prioritize potential causes based on their significance and likelihood of contributing to the problem.

5. **Data Analysis:** Analyze data and evidence to verify the selected causes' involvement in the problem.

6. **Root Cause Identification:** Through analysis and verification, identify the root cause or causes of the problem.

7. **Preventive Action Planning:** Develop and implement preventive actions to eliminate or mitigate the root cause and prevent future occurrences.

8. **Monitoring and Validation:** Continuously monitor the effectiveness of preventive actions and validate that the problem does not recur.

Benefits of Root Cause Analysis:

1. **Problem Resolution:** RCA addresses problems at their source, leading to more effective and lasting solutions.

2. **Preventive Action:** Identifying and addressing root causes helps prevent future occurrences of the same problem.

3. **Efficiency:** RCA streamlines processes by eliminating unnecessary steps or identifying process improvements.

4. **Cost Reduction:** By preventing issues and minimizing rework, RCA reduces costs associated with defects or problems.

5. **Enhanced Quality:** RCA contributes to improved product or service quality, leading to higher customer satisfaction.

Challenges in Root Cause Analysis:

1. **Complexity:** Some problems have multiple root causes, making it challenging to identify and address them all effectively.

2. **Data Availability:** RCA requires access to relevant data, and in some cases, data may be incomplete or unavailable.

3. **Subjectivity:** The effectiveness of RCA can be influenced by the team's subjectivity and assumptions.

4. **Resource Intensive:** Conducting a thorough RCA can be time-consuming and may require significant resources.

In conclusion, Root Cause Analysis is a systematic and structured approach to identifying and addressing the underlying causes of problems or defects. It is a fundamental practice in quality management, aimed at preventing the recurrence of issues and enhancing overall product or service quality. By using various methodologies and tools, organizations can uncover root causes, implement preventive actions, and foster a culture of continuous improvement. Root Cause Analysis plays a pivotal role in quality assurance, helping organizations deliver consistent quality and meet customer expectations.

E. Nonconformance Management

Nonconformance management is a critical aspect of quality control and quality assurance, focusing on the identification, documentation, evaluation, and resolution of nonconformities or deviations from established quality standards, specifications, or requirements. This section provides an in-depth exploration of nonconformance management, its processes, methodologies, and its vital role in maintaining and enhancing product or service quality.

Key Concepts in Nonconformance Management:

1. **Nonconformance:** A nonconformance refers to any instance where a product, process, or service does not meet specified quality standards, requirements, or specifications.

2. **Root Cause Analysis:** Identifying and addressing the root causes of nonconformities is fundamental to preventing their recurrence.

3. **Corrective Action:** Corrective actions are measures taken to rectify nonconformities and prevent their recurrence.

4. **Preventive Action:** Preventive actions are proactive measures implemented to prevent potential nonconformities.

5. **Documentation:** Accurate and thorough documentation of nonconformities, investigations, and corrective actions is essential for traceability and compliance.

Nonconformance Management Process:

1. **Identification:** Nonconformities can be identified through various means, including inspections, audits, customer complaints, or internal reports.

2. **Documentation:** Once identified, nonconformities are documented in detail. This documentation typically includes the nature of the nonconformance, its location, date of

occurrence, and individuals involved.

3. **Evaluation:** Nonconformities are evaluated to determine their significance and potential impact on product quality or safety. A risk assessment may be conducted.

4. **Root Cause Analysis:** To prevent recurrence, root cause analysis is performed to identify the underlying reasons for the nonconformance.

5. **Corrective Actions:** Corrective actions are developed and implemented to address the nonconformance's root causes, ensuring it is rectified.

6. **Verification:** The effectiveness of corrective actions is verified through testing, inspection, or other suitable means to confirm that the nonconformance has been resolved.

7. **Preventive Actions:** To prevent similar issues from occurring in the future, preventive actions may be identified and implemented.

8. **Closure:** Once nonconformities have been addressed and verified, they can be closed, and the documentation is archived.

Tools and Techniques in Nonconformance Management:

1. **Root Cause Analysis Tools:** Tools like the 5 Whys, Fishbone

(Ishikawa) diagrams, and fault tree analysis are used to identify the root causes of nonconformities.

2. **Corrective Action Plans:** Detailed plans outlining the steps, responsibilities, and timelines for implementing corrective actions.

3. **Preventive Action Plans:** Proactive plans to prevent the recurrence of nonconformities in the future.

4. **Risk Assessment:** Assessing the potential impact and severity of nonconformities to prioritize corrective and preventive actions.

5. **Quality Management Software:** Software solutions facilitate the documentation, tracking, and management of nonconformances and related actions.

Benefits of Nonconformance Management:

1. **Quality Improvement:** Nonconformance management leads to continuous quality improvement by identifying and addressing issues at their source.

2. **Customer Satisfaction:** Resolving nonconformities ensures that products or services meet or exceed customer expectations.

3. **Efficiency:** Efficient nonconformance management reduces

waste, rework, and costs associated with defects.

4. **Compliance:** Ensuring that products and processes conform to quality standards and regulations.

5. **Risk Mitigation:** Identifying and addressing nonconformities reduces the risk of product recalls, safety incidents, or legal issues.

Challenges in Nonconformance Management:

1. **Timeliness:** Delays in identifying, documenting, or resolving nonconformities can lead to more significant problems.

2. **Data Accuracy:** Ensuring the accuracy and completeness of nonconformance data is crucial for effective analysis.

3. **Resistance to Change:** Resistance within the organization can hinder the adoption of nonconformance management processes.

4. **Complexity:** Complex nonconformities may require extensive investigation and multiple corrective actions.

In conclusion, nonconformance management is a systematic and structured approach to identifying, addressing, and preventing nonconformities in products, processes, or services. It plays a pivotal role in quality control and quality assurance, contributing to the delivery of consistent quality, customer satisfaction, and compliance with industry standards and regulations. Nonconformance management promotes a culture of continuous improvement, risk mitigation, and proactive problem-solving within organizations.

CHAPTER 6

Quality Tools and Techniques

Quality Tools and Techniques are a set of systematic and structured approaches, methodologies, and instruments employed in quality management to analyze, monitor, improve, and control processes and products. These tools and techniques are indispensable in identifying and addressing quality issues, enhancing efficiency, and achieving high levels of product or service quality. In this section, we will explore various quality tools and techniques that organizations utilize to foster a culture of continuous improvement and ensure that quality standards are met consistently across industries and sectors.

A. Identifying the Vital Few

Pareto Analysis, often referred to as the 80/20 rule, is a powerful quality tool that helps organizations prioritize and focus their efforts on the most critical factors contributing to a problem or achieving a desired outcome. Named after the Italian economist Vilfredo Pareto, this technique is based on the observation that a significant majority of effects (approximately 80%) often result from a minority of causes (approximately 20%). In-depth knowledge of Pareto Analysis is crucial for quality management and process improvement.

Key Principles of Pareto Analysis:

1. **Focus on the Vital Few:** Pareto Analysis emphasizes identifying and addressing the most influential factors or issues that have the most significant impact on a problem or objective.

2. **Quantitative Approach:** Data and quantitative analysis drive Pareto Analysis, making it an objective and data-driven tool.

3. **Prioritization:** The primary goal is to prioritize resources, time, and efforts on the most critical areas for improvement.

Steps in Performing Pareto Analysis:

1. **Define the Problem or Objective:** Clearly articulate the problem or objective you want to address. This could be related to quality issues, process improvement, customer complaints, or any area where prioritization is necessary.

2. **Data Collection:** Gather relevant data that describe the various factors or categories associated with the problem or objective. Ensure that the data is accurate and representative.

3. **Data Sorting and Analysis:** Organize the data into categories and calculate the frequency or occurrence of each category.

Determine the cumulative percentage of the categories.

4. **Create a Pareto Chart:** Construct a Pareto chart, which is a bar graph where categories are listed on the x-axis in descending order of frequency, and the corresponding frequencies or occurrences are represented by the height of the bars on the y-axis. The cumulative percentage line is also plotted on the chart.

5. **Identify the Vital Few:** Analyze the Pareto chart to identify the categories that contribute to the majority of the problem or objective's effects. These are the vital few.

6. **Prioritize Actions:** Focus your efforts on addressing the vital few categories. These are the areas where interventions are likely to have the most significant impact.

Benefits of Pareto Analysis:

1. **Efficient Resource Allocation:** Pareto Analysis helps organizations allocate resources, time, and efforts efficiently by concentrating on the most influential factors.

2. **Effective Problem Solving:** It guides problem-solving efforts to target the root causes or issues that matter the most.

3. **Improved Decision Making:** Pareto charts provide clear, data-driven insights that support better decision-making in various areas, from quality improvement to project

management.

4. **Quick Results:** Addressing the vital few can lead to rapid improvements and immediate positive outcomes.

5. **Prioritization:** Pareto Analysis helps teams prioritize actions and avoid spreading resources too thinly across numerous issues.

Challenges in Pareto Analysis:

1. **Data Accuracy:** The accuracy of data used in Pareto Analysis is crucial. Inaccurate or incomplete data can lead to incorrect prioritization.

2. **Subjectivity:** Deciding what constitutes a category and how data is categorized can introduce subjectivity into the analysis.

3. **Changing Factors:** The relevance of factors and their contribution to a problem can change over time, requiring regular updates to the analysis.

4. **Overlooking Less Frequent Factors:** Focusing exclusively on the vital few may cause organizations to overlook less frequent but still important factors.

Applications of Pareto Analysis:

1. **Quality Improvement:** In quality management, Pareto Analysis is used to identify the most frequent quality issues

and prioritize corrective actions.

2. **Customer Complaints:** Organizations can use Pareto Analysis to determine the most common reasons for customer complaints and take steps to address them.

3. **Inventory Management:** It can help in managing inventory by identifying the most critical items that need close monitoring.

4. **Project Management:** Pareto Analysis assists project managers in identifying and addressing the most significant project bottlenecks or risks.

5. **Sales and Marketing:** In sales and marketing, it can help identify the products, markets, or channels that generate the most revenue or contribute most to profitability.

In conclusion, Pareto Analysis is a valuable tool for quality management, problem-solving, and resource allocation. By focusing on the vital few factors that have the most significant impact, organizations can make informed decisions, allocate resources efficiently, and achieve substantial improvements in quality and performance. Pareto Analysis is a cornerstone technique in quality management and process improvement, helping organizations address their most pressing issues systematically and effectively.

B. Fishbone Diagram (Ishikawa): Analyzing Causes and Effects

The Fishbone Diagram, also known as the Ishikawa Diagram or Cause-and-Effect Diagram, is a visual tool used for systematically identifying and analyzing the root causes of a problem or an effect. Developed by Japanese quality control expert Kaoru Ishikawa, this technique helps organizations uncover the underlying factors contributing to issues and facilitates problem-solving and quality improvement efforts. In this section, we will explore the in-depth concepts and applications of the Fishbone Diagram.

Anatomy of a Fishbone Diagram:

A Fishbone Diagram gets its name from its visual resemblance to a fish's skeleton, with the "head" representing the problem or effect, and the "bones" representing different categories of potential causes. The main components of a Fishbone Diagram include:

1. **Problem or Effect:** At the "head" of the diagram, clearly state the problem or effect you are investigating. This is the issue you want to analyze.

2. **Spine:** The spine is a horizontal line extending from the problem statement, connecting the "head" to the "bones."

3. **Bones:** These are the categories of potential causes that can

contribute to the problem or effect. Commonly used categories, often known as the "5Ms and 1P," include:

- **Manpower (People):** Factors related to human resources, such as skills, training, or staffing levels.

- **Machinery (Equipment):** Factors related to equipment, tools, and technology.

- **Methods:** Process-related factors, including procedures, standards, or work methods.

- **Materials:** Factors related to raw materials, components, or supplies.

- **Measurement:** Factors related to data collection, quality metrics, or measurement tools.

- **Environment (Place):** Factors related to the physical environment, workspace conditions, or external influences.

Steps in Creating a Fishbone Diagram:

1. **Define the Problem or Effect:** Clearly articulate the problem or effect you want to investigate. This serves as the "head" of the diagram.

2. **Identify Categories (Bones):** Determine the appropriate categories of potential causes that may contribute to the

problem. These categories are the "bones" of the diagram.

3. **Brainstorm Causes:** Within each category, brainstorm possible causes or factors that could be contributing to the problem. Encourage input from team members or stakeholders.

4. **Construct the Diagram:** Draw the Fishbone Diagram by connecting the "head" (problem or effect) to the "bones" (categories) using the spine. Each cause within a category is represented as smaller lines extending from the corresponding bone.

5. **Analyze and Prioritize:** Review the diagram to identify the most likely and impactful causes within each category. Prioritize the causes for further investigation.

6. **Investigate Root Causes:** For the prioritized causes, conduct root cause analysis to determine the underlying reasons or factors contributing to the problem.

7. **Develop Solutions:** Based on the root causes identified, develop and implement solutions to address the problem.

Benefits of Fishbone Diagram (Ishikawa):

1. **Visual Clarity:** The diagram provides a clear and structured visual representation of causes and their relationships, making complex issues more understandable.

2. **Systematic Analysis:** It encourages a systematic approach to problem-solving by categorizing causes and facilitating brainstorming.

3. **Cross-Functional Collaboration:** Teams from various departments can collaborate effectively in identifying causes and solutions.

4. **Focus on Root Causes:** The technique helps organizations focus on addressing root causes rather than symptoms, leading to long-term solutions.

5. **Continuous Improvement:** It supports a culture of continuous improvement by promoting structured problem-solving and learning from past issues.

Challenges in Using Fishbone Diagrams:

1. **Subjectivity:** The effectiveness of the diagram can be influenced by the subjectivity of cause identification and prioritization.

2. **Complexity:** In situations with numerous potential causes, the diagram can become complex and challenging to manage.

3. **Time-Consuming:** The process of brainstorming, constructing the diagram, and investigating root causes can be time-consuming.

Applications of Fishbone Diagrams:

1. **Quality Improvement:** Fishbone diagrams are widely used in quality management to analyze defects, deviations, or variations in processes or products.

2. **Problem Solving:** They help identify the root causes of operational or performance problems and guide corrective actions.

3. **Product Design:** In product development, they can be used to evaluate design-related issues and optimize product features.

4. **Service Improvement:** Fishbone diagrams are applicable to service industries for analyzing service quality, customer complaints, and process inefficiencies.

5. **Risk Analysis:** They are employed in risk management to assess potential risks and their underlying causes.

In conclusion, the Fishbone Diagram (Ishikawa) is a valuable tool for identifying and analyzing the causes of problems or effects systematically. By categorizing causes and visually representing their relationships, organizations can prioritize and address the most critical factors contributing to issues. This structured approach to problem-solving and quality improvement contributes to enhanced product or service quality, increased efficiency, and a culture of continuous improvement within organizations.

C. 5 Whys Analysis: Uncovering the Root Causes of Problems

The 5 Whys Analysis is a straightforward yet powerful problem-solving technique that seeks to identify the root causes of an issue by repeatedly asking the question "Why?" Each successive "Why?" delves deeper into the problem, uncovering not just the symptoms but also the underlying factors that contribute to it. Developed in Japan as part of the Toyota Production System, the 5 Whys Analysis is widely used in quality management, process improvement, and root cause analysis.

Key Principles of the 5 Whys Analysis:

1. **Root Cause Focus:** The primary goal is to identify the fundamental or root causes of a problem, not just the superficial symptoms.

2. **Systematic Approach:** The process involves asking "Why?" repeatedly, typically five times, to dig deeper into the issue and explore causality.

3. **Team Collaboration:** It is often performed in a team setting, encouraging input from individuals with diverse perspectives and expertise.

4. **Data-Driven:** The analysis is based on factual data and observations rather than assumptions or opinions.

Steps in Conducting a 5 Whys Analysis:

1. **Define the Problem:** Clearly define the problem or issue you want to address. It's essential to have a precise problem statement to begin the analysis.

2. **Ask the First "Why?":** Start by asking why the problem occurred. This will lead you to an immediate cause or factor contributing to the issue.

3. **Repeat the Process:** For each answer to the previous "Why?" question, ask "Why?" again. Continue this process for approximately five iterations or until you reach a point where further "Whys" do not yield meaningful answers.

4. **Analyze and Identify Root Causes:** Review the answers to the "Why?" questions. The point where you can no longer ask "Why?" and the answers indicate the root causes of the problem.

5. **Develop Solutions:** Once you've identified the root causes, brainstorm and implement corrective actions or solutions to address these causes directly.

Benefits of the 5 Whys Analysis:

1. **Root Cause Identification:** The technique is highly effective in pinpointing the true underlying causes of problems.

2. **Cost-Effective:** It is a simple and low-cost method that doesn't require elaborate tools or resources.

3. **Quick Results:** The 5 Whys Analysis can lead to rapid problem resolution, as it focuses on addressing the root causes.

4. **Preventive Action:** By addressing root causes, the technique helps prevent the recurrence of the same problem in the future.

5. **Enhanced Understanding:** It deepens the understanding of complex issues by breaking them down into simpler, more manageable components.

Challenges in Conducting 5 Whys Analysis:

1. **Subjectivity:** The effectiveness of the analysis can be influenced by the subjectivity of individuals involved and their assumptions.

2. **Limited Scope:** The technique may not be suitable for extremely complex problems that involve multiple interacting factors.

3. **Cultural Barriers:** In some organizational cultures, people may be hesitant to ask "Why?" repeatedly or explore root causes due to fear of blame.

Applications of the 5 Whys Analysis:

1. **Quality Improvement:** It is widely used in quality

management to identify and address defects or variations in processes and products.

2. **Safety Investigations:** In safety management, the technique helps uncover the root causes of accidents or incidents.

3. **Process Improvement:** The 5 Whys can be applied to optimize processes, reduce waste, and enhance efficiency.

4. **Customer Complaints:** It is useful for investigating customer complaints and improving customer satisfaction.

5. **Problem Solving:** It is a valuable tool for general problem-solving across various industries and sectors.

In conclusion, the 5 Whys Analysis is a valuable and accessible technique for uncovering the root causes of problems and driving effective problem-solving and improvement efforts. By asking "Why?" repeatedly and delving deeper into the issue, organizations can identify and address the fundamental factors contributing to problems, leading to better quality, increased efficiency, and enhanced problem-solving capabilities.

D. Process Capability Analysis: Ensuring Quality and Consistency

Process Capability Analysis is a statistical methodology used in quality management and manufacturing to assess and quantify the ability of a process to consistently produce products or services that meet specified requirements and standards. This technique is crucial for organizations striving for continuous improvement, quality control, and meeting customer expectations consistently. In this section, we will explore the in-depth concepts and applications of Process Capability Analysis.

Key Principles of Process Capability Analysis:

1. **Customer-Centric:** The focus is on meeting customer requirements and delivering products or services that align with customer expectations.

2. **Statistical Approach:** Process Capability Analysis employs statistical tools and methods to assess process performance and variation.

3. **Data-Driven:** It relies on data collected from the process to make informed assessments and decisions.

4. **Predictive:** By analyzing process capability, organizations can predict the likelihood of products or services meeting specifications.

Common Metrics in Process Capability Analysis:

1. **Process Capability Index (Cp):** Cp measures the capability of a process to produce products or services within specified tolerances. A higher Cp value indicates a more capable

process.

2. **Process Capability Ratio (Cpk):** Cpk considers both the process variability and the distance between the process mean and specification limits. It provides a more comprehensive view of process capability.

3. **Process Performance Index (Pp):** Pp is similar to Cp but is used when the process is centered within the specification limits. It assesses how well the process can perform within its natural variation.

4. **Process Performance Ratio (Ppk):** Ppk, like Cpk, accounts for process centering but provides a more complete assessment of performance.

Steps in Conducting Process Capability Analysis:

1. **Define the Process:** Clearly define the process to be analyzed, including the inputs, outputs, and specifications.

2. **Data Collection:** Gather data from the process, including measurements or observations of the product or service characteristics.

3. **Calculate Process Capability Indices:** Use the collected data to calculate the appropriate process capability indices (Cp, Cpk, Pp, Ppk).

4. **Interpret the Results:** Evaluate the process capability indices to determine how well the process is performing relative to the specification limits.

5. **Compare with Specifications:** Compare the process capability indices to the customer's or organization's specified tolerances to assess whether the process meets requirements.

6. **Continuous Improvement:** If the process capability falls short of requirements, take corrective actions to improve the process and monitor the impact of these changes.

Benefits of Process Capability Analysis:

1. **Quality Assurance:** It ensures that products or services consistently meet quality standards and customer requirements.

2. **Reduced Defects:** By quantifying process capability, organizations can reduce defects and variations in their products or services.

3. **Customer Satisfaction:** Meeting specifications consistently leads to higher customer satisfaction and loyalty.

4. **Cost Reduction:** Process capability analysis can help identify and eliminate waste and inefficiencies, leading to cost savings.

5. **Data-Driven Decision Making:** It provides data-driven

insights for making informed decisions about process improvements.

Challenges in Process Capability Analysis:

1. **Data Availability:** Adequate and accurate data are essential for meaningful process capability analysis. Data collection can be challenging in some cases.

2. **Process Complexity:** Highly complex processes may require advanced statistical techniques and expertise for accurate analysis.

3. **Dynamic Processes:** Processes that change frequently may require continuous monitoring and adjustment of process capability.

Applications of Process Capability Analysis:

1. **Manufacturing:** It is extensively used in manufacturing industries to assess the capability of production processes, ensuring that products meet quality standards.

2. **Service Industries:** Process capability analysis is also applicable in service industries to assess the consistency of service delivery.

3. **Healthcare:** In healthcare, it is used to evaluate and improve medical processes and ensure patient safety.

4. **Software Development:** In software development, it can be applied to assess the capability of development and testing processes.

5. **Supply Chain Management:** Process capability analysis helps ensure that suppliers meet quality and performance standards.

In conclusion, Process Capability Analysis is a vital tool for organizations aiming to consistently deliver high-quality products or services that meet customer requirements. By quantifying process performance and assessing its alignment with specifications, organizations can identify areas for improvement, reduce defects, and enhance customer satisfaction. This data-driven approach to quality management and process improvement is fundamental in today's competitive business environment.

E. Design of Experiments (DOE): Optimizing Processes and Products

Design of Experiments (DOE) is a systematic and structured methodology used in various industries and fields to plan, conduct, and analyze experiments aimed at optimizing processes, products, and systems. DOE enables organizations to efficiently explore and understand the impact of multiple variables on an outcome, identify optimal conditions, and make data-driven decisions to improve quality, efficiency, and performance. In this section, we will delve into the in-depth concepts and applications of Design of Experiments.

Key Principles of Design of Experiments:

1. **Systematic Variation:** DOE systematically varies input factors (independent variables) to observe their effects on the output (dependent variable).

2. **Control and Randomization:** Careful control and randomization of experimental conditions minimize bias and ensure reliable results.

3. **Replication:** Replicating experiments helps verify results and assess the consistency of outcomes.

4. **Statistical Analysis:** Statistical tools and techniques are employed to analyze data and draw conclusions from experiments.

Steps in Conducting Design of Experiments:

1. **Define the Objective:** Clearly define the objective of the experiment, including the response variable (what you want to optimize) and the factors or variables to be studied.

2. **Identify Factors and Levels:** Identify the independent factors that may influence the response variable and define the levels at which each factor will be tested.

3. **Experimental Design:** Choose an appropriate experimental design, such as factorial design, response surface methodology, or Taguchi method, based on the nature of the problem and the number of factors.

4. **Plan and Conduct Experiments:** Design and execute the experiments according to the chosen design, systematically varying factors and recording responses.

5. **Collect Data:** Collect data on the responses and factors while ensuring accuracy and consistency.

6. **Data Analysis:** Use statistical analysis techniques to analyze the data, including analysis of variance (ANOVA), regression analysis, and graphical methods.

7. **Interpret Results:** Interpret the results to identify significant factors, interactions, and optimal conditions for the response variable.

8. **Optimization:** Based on the analysis, identify the conditions or settings that optimize the response variable and achieve the desired outcome.

9. **Validation and Implementation:** Verify the optimized conditions through additional experiments or validation studies and implement the findings into the process or product.

Benefits of Design of Experiments:

1. **Efficiency:** DOE allows organizations to achieve results with fewer experiments compared to one-factor-at-a-time testing, saving time and resources.

2. **Data-Driven Decision Making:** It provides empirical evidence and data-driven insights for making informed decisions about process or product optimization.

3. **Optimization:** DOE helps identify the optimal settings for factors, leading to improved quality, efficiency, and performance.

4. **Understanding Complex Systems:** It aids in understanding the complex interactions among multiple factors in a system.

5. **Risk Reduction:** By systematically exploring factors and interactions, DOE reduces the risk of unexpected issues during process or product development.

Challenges in Design of Experiments:

1. **Expertise:** Properly planning and conducting DOE requires expertise in statistical methods and experimental design.

2. **Resource Intensive:** Conducting experiments and data analysis can be resource-intensive, especially in complex systems.

3. **External Factors:** Experiments may be influenced by external factors or uncontrolled variables.

Applications of Design of Experiments:

1. **Manufacturing:** In manufacturing, DOE is used to optimize production processes, improve product quality, and reduce defects.

2. **Product Development:** In product development, it helps design and refine products to meet performance specifications.

3. **Pharmaceuticals:** Pharmaceutical companies use DOE to optimize drug formulations, manufacturing processes, and quality control.

4. **Chemical Engineering:** In chemical engineering, it aids in process optimization, chemical reaction studies, and product formulation.

5. **Agriculture:** Agriculture benefits from DOE in optimizing crop yields, fertilizer application, and pest control.

6. **Healthcare:** In healthcare, it is used to optimize treatment protocols, clinical trials, and medical device design.

7. **Marketing and Advertising:** DOE can be applied to optimize marketing campaigns, pricing strategies, and product placement.

In conclusion, Design of Experiments is a powerful methodology for systematically optimizing processes, products, and systems by exploring the effects of multiple variables. Its data-driven approach, supported by statistical analysis, helps organizations make informed decisions to improve quality, efficiency, and performance. DOE is a valuable tool in research, development, and problem-solving across various industries, contributing to innovation and continuous improvement.

F. Failure Mode and Effects Analysis (FMEA): Enhancing Reliability and Safety

Failure Mode and Effects Analysis (FMEA) is a structured and systematic approach used across various industries to identify and prioritize potential failure modes, assess their effects, and develop mitigation strategies to enhance reliability, safety, and quality. FMEA is a proactive tool that helps organizations prevent or mitigate failures before they occur, reducing risks and improving overall performance. In this section, we will explore the in-depth concepts and applications of Failure Mode and Effects Analysis.

Key Principles of Failure Mode and Effects Analysis (FMEA):

1. **Systematic Evaluation:** FMEA systematically assesses potential failure modes, their causes, effects, and criticality.

2. **Preventive Approach:** It focuses on identifying and addressing failure modes before they lead to adverse consequences.

3. **Cross-Functional Collaboration:** FMEA typically involves cross-functional teams with diverse expertise to gather comprehensive insights.

4. **Risk Prioritization:** The analysis assigns risk priorities to failure modes based on severity, occurrence, and detectability.

Steps in Conducting Failure Mode and Effects Analysis (FMEA):

1. **Select the System or Process:** Identify the system, product, process, or component to be analyzed using FMEA.

2. **Assemble a Cross-Functional Team:** Form a team with members representing various functions and expertise related to the system or process.

3. **Define the Scope:** Clearly define the scope of the FMEA, including its objectives, boundaries, and the level of detail to be analyzed.

4. **Identify Failure Modes:** List all potential failure modes— ways in which the system or process may fail.

5. **Determine Causes and Effects:** For each failure mode,

identify the causes or mechanisms that can lead to it and the potential effects or consequences of the failure.

6. **Assign Severity Ratings:** Rate the severity of each failure mode's potential effects on a scale (e.g., 1 to 10), considering safety, regulatory compliance, customer satisfaction, and other relevant factors.

7. **Assign Occurrence Ratings:** Rate the likelihood or occurrence of each failure mode on a scale (e.g., 1 to 10), considering historical data, expert opinions, and analysis.

8. **Assign Detection Ratings:** Rate the likelihood of detecting each failure mode before it reaches the customer or causes harm on a scale (e.g., 1 to 10).

9. **Calculate Risk Priority Numbers (RPNs):** Multiply the severity, occurrence, and detection ratings for each failure mode to calculate its RPN. The RPN is used to prioritize failure modes.

10. **Prioritize and Develop Mitigation Strategies:** Prioritize failure modes based on their RPNs. Focus on high-risk failure modes and develop mitigation strategies to reduce their RPNs.

11. **Implement Mitigation Measures:** Implement the identified mitigation measures and track their effectiveness in reducing risks.

12. **Reevaluate and Update:** Periodically reevaluate the FMEA to account for changes in the system, new risks, or the effectiveness of mitigation strategies.

Benefits of Failure Mode and Effects Analysis (FMEA):

1. **Risk Reduction:** FMEA helps organizations proactively identify and mitigate risks, reducing the likelihood of failures and their consequences.

2. **Improved Safety:** It enhances safety by identifying potential hazards and addressing them before they lead to accidents or harm.

3. **Quality Improvement:** FMEA contributes to improved product or process quality by addressing failure modes that can lead to defects.

4. **Cost Savings:** By preventing failures, organizations can avoid costly rework, recalls, warranty claims, and legal liabilities.

5. **Enhanced Reliability:** FMEA improves the reliability and performance of systems and processes.

Challenges in Conducting Failure Mode and Effects Analysis (FMEA):

1. **Data Availability:** Availability of accurate data on failure modes, causes, and effects is crucial for meaningful FMEA.

2. **Subjectivity:** Ratings assigned to severity, occurrence, and detection can be subjective and may vary among team members.

3. **Resource Intensive:** Conducting FMEA can be time-consuming, especially for complex systems or processes.

Applications of Failure Mode and Effects Analysis (FMEA):

1. **Manufacturing:** FMEA is widely used in manufacturing to assess and mitigate risks in production processes, reducing defects and improving quality.

2. **Aerospace and Automotive Industries:** These industries use FMEA extensively to enhance the safety and reliability of their products.

3. **Healthcare:** FMEA is applied in healthcare to assess risks in medical processes, patient care, and the development of medical devices.

4. **Engineering and Design:** It helps engineers and designers identify and address potential failures in product design and development.

5. **Energy Sector:** FMEA is used to assess risks in power generation, transmission, and distribution systems.

6. **Pharmaceuticals:** In the pharmaceutical industry, FMEA is employed to ensure drug safety and product quality.

7. **Software Development:** FMEA can be adapted to assess risks in software development processes and improve software reliability.

In conclusion, Failure Mode and Effects Analysis (FMEA) is a valuable tool for organizations seeking to proactively manage risks, enhance safety, and improve quality and reliability. By systematically analyzing potential failure modes and their consequences, FMEA allows organizations to take preventive actions and reduce the likelihood of costly failures and their associated impacts. It is a critical component of quality management and risk mitigation in various industries.

CHAPTER 7

Total Quality Management (TQM)

Total Quality Management (TQM) is a comprehensive and integrated management philosophy that emphasizes continuous improvement, customer focus, and the involvement of all employees in an organization's quest for excellence. TQM is not just a set of tools or techniques; it's a cultural shift that permeates an organization from top to bottom, fostering a commitment to delivering the highest quality products or services and achieving long-term success. In this introductory section, we'll explore the fundamental principles and concepts of Total Quality Management.

A. Total Quality Management (TQM) Principles and Practices: Pursuing Excellence

Total Quality Management (TQM) is a holistic approach to organizational management that prioritizes quality and customer satisfaction. TQM is not a mere set of tools or techniques; rather, it represents a fundamental shift in how organizations operate, emphasizing continuous improvement, customer focus, and the involvement of all employees. In this section, we will delve into the in-depth principles and practices that underpin the philosophy of Total Quality Management.

Key TQM Principles:

1. **Customer Focus:** The primary focus of TQM is meeting and exceeding customer expectations. This principle emphasizes the need to understand customer needs, preferences, and feedback to deliver products or services that consistently satisfy them.

2. **Continuous Improvement:** TQM advocates a never-ending quest for improvement in all aspects of the organization. This principle is often embodied by the Japanese concept of "Kaizen," which encourages small, incremental improvements over time.

3. **Employee Involvement:** TQM recognizes that employees are the backbone of an organization. It encourages the active participation and empowerment of employees at all levels to contribute their expertise and ideas to improve processes and quality.

4. **Process-Centric Approach:** TQM emphasizes the importance of well-defined processes. Organizations are encouraged to document, analyze, and continuously improve their processes to eliminate inefficiencies and defects.

5. **Data-Driven Decision Making:** Data and facts should drive decision-making. TQM promotes the collection and analysis of data to make informed decisions and monitor the performance of processes and products.

6. **Supplier Partnerships:** TQM extends beyond the organization's boundaries to include suppliers. Building strong, collaborative relationships with suppliers ensures the quality of incoming materials and components.

7. **Leadership Commitment:** Leadership plays a pivotal role in TQM implementation. Top management must demonstrate a visible and unwavering commitment to quality and lead by example.

8. **Strategic Approach:** TQM aligns quality efforts with the organization's strategic goals. It ensures that quality is not treated as a separate function but is integrated into the overall strategic planning.

Key TQM Practices:

1. **Quality Planning:** Organizations must proactively plan for quality by setting clear quality objectives, standards, and guidelines. This includes defining quality characteristics and customer expectations.

2. **Quality Control:** TQM employs rigorous quality control

measures to ensure that products or services meet established standards. Techniques like Statistical Process Control (SPC) are commonly used for this purpose.

3. **Quality Improvement:** Continuous improvement efforts are essential to TQM. Teams use methods like Kaizen, Six Sigma, and Lean to identify and eliminate defects and waste.

4. **Training and Education:** Employees receive training to enhance their skills and knowledge, empowering them to contribute effectively to quality improvement initiatives.

5. **Employee Involvement:** TQM encourages employees to participate in quality circles, problem-solving teams, and suggestion programs. This involvement fosters a sense of ownership and responsibility for quality.

6. **Process Management:** Well-documented and standardized processes are critical to TQM. Process management involves mapping, analyzing, and optimizing processes to ensure consistency and quality.

7. **Customer Feedback:** Organizations actively seek and collect customer feedback to understand their needs and expectations. Customer feedback is used to drive improvements in products and services.

8. **Benchmarking:** TQM involves benchmarking against

industry best practices and competitors to identify areas for improvement and set performance standards.

9. **Supplier Relationships:** TQM extends to suppliers, fostering long-term relationships based on trust and mutual benefit. Organizations work closely with suppliers to ensure the quality of incoming materials and components.

10. **Measurement and Analysis:** Data collection and analysis are integral to TQM. Key performance indicators (KPIs) and statistical analysis are used to monitor processes and make informed decisions.

Benefits of TQM:

1. **Enhanced Customer Satisfaction:** By focusing on customer needs and continuously improving products and services, TQM leads to higher customer satisfaction and loyalty.

2. **Improved Quality:** TQM reduces defects and errors, resulting in higher product and service quality.

3. **Efficiency and Cost Reduction:** Streamlining processes and eliminating waste leads to increased efficiency and cost savings.

4. **Employee Morale:** Employee involvement and empowerment in TQM efforts improve morale and job satisfaction.

5. **Competitive Advantage:** TQM helps organizations gain a competitive edge by delivering superior quality and value to customers.

6. **Long-Term Sustainability:** TQM promotes a culture of excellence and continuous improvement, contributing to an organization's long-term sustainability.

In conclusion, Total Quality Management (TQM) represents a holistic approach to organizational excellence, emphasizing customer focus, continuous improvement, employee involvement, and data-driven decision-making. TQM principles and practices are instrumental in achieving and maintaining high-quality products and services, ensuring customer satisfaction, and driving organizational success. TQM is not just a set of practices but a cultural transformation that can lead to lasting competitiveness and excellence.

B. Customer Focus in Total Quality Management (TQM): Meeting and Exceeding Expectations

Customer focus is a central tenet of Total Quality Management (TQM), emphasizing that organizations exist to meet customer needs and exceed customer expectations. In TQM, the customer is at the forefront of all decision-making processes and quality improvement efforts. This focus on the customer is not limited to external customers but extends to internal customers, such as employees and departments within the organization. In this section, we will explore the in-depth concepts and practices of customer focus within TQM.

Understanding Customer Focus in TQM:

1. **External Customers:** These are the end-users or consumers of an organization's products or services. TQM recognizes the importance of understanding their needs, preferences, and expectations.

2. **Internal Customers:** In a broader sense, internal customers refer to individuals or departments within the organization who rely on the output of other departments. For example, the finance department is an internal customer of the procurement department. TQM emphasizes the need for seamless internal processes to meet the needs of these internal customers.

Key Practices for Customer Focus in TQM:

1. **Customer Needs Assessment:** Organizations must actively seek to understand customer needs and expectations through methods such as surveys, feedback forms, focus groups, and market research.

2. **Voice of the Customer (VoC):** VoC is a structured approach to capturing, analyzing, and acting on customer feedback. It

ensures that customer opinions and preferences drive decision-making.

3. **Quality Function Deployment (QFD):** QFD is a systematic process that translates customer needs and expectations into specific product or service design requirements.

4. **Customer Relationship Management (CRM):** CRM systems and practices help organizations manage and nurture relationships with customers, ensuring personalized interactions and addressing their concerns promptly.

5. **Complaint Handling:** Organizations should have effective mechanisms for receiving, tracking, and resolving customer complaints. The goal is not only to resolve issues but also to prevent their recurrence.

6. **Continuous Improvement:** TQM's principle of continuous improvement applies to customer focus as well. Organizations must continuously strive to enhance their products and services based on changing customer needs and market dynamics.

Benefits of Customer Focus in TQM:

1. **Enhanced Customer Satisfaction:** By understanding and meeting customer needs and expectations, organizations can significantly increase customer satisfaction and loyalty.

2. **Increased Market Share:** Satisfied customers are more likely to become loyal customers and refer others to the organization, leading to an expanded market share.

3. **Product and Service Improvement:** Customer feedback drives continuous improvement efforts, resulting in better products and services.

4. **Competitive Advantage:** Organizations that consistently deliver on customer expectations gain a competitive edge in the market.

5. **Reduced Customer Churn:** High customer satisfaction reduces the likelihood of customers switching to competitors.

6. **Innovation:** Customer-focused organizations are more innovative, as they proactively respond to changing customer needs and preferences.

Challenges in Maintaining Customer Focus:

1. **Changing Customer Needs:** Customer needs and preferences can evolve rapidly. Organizations must stay attuned to these changes to remain customer-focused.

2. **Balancing Stakeholder Interests:** Organizations often have multiple stakeholders with diverse interests. Balancing these interests while maintaining customer focus can be challenging.

3. **Resource Allocation:** Allocating resources to customer-focused initiatives, such as market research and complaint handling, can be resource-intensive.

4. **Internal Resistance:** Not all employees may initially embrace a customer-centric approach. Overcoming internal resistance and fostering a customer-focused culture requires leadership commitment and effective communication.

Integrating Customer Focus into TQM:

To integrate customer focus effectively into TQM, organizations should:

1. **Set Clear Objectives:** Establish clear and measurable objectives related to customer satisfaction and retention.

2. **Implement Customer-Centric Processes:** Ensure that customer-focused practices are integrated into all organizational processes, from product development to service delivery.

3. **Foster a Culture of Customer Focus:** Create a culture that values customer feedback, encourages innovation, and empowers employees to take ownership of customer satisfaction.

4. **Monitor and Measure:** Continuously monitor customer satisfaction through metrics, surveys, and feedback

mechanisms, and use this data to drive improvements.

5. **Provide Training:** Educate employees at all levels about the importance of customer focus and provide training on customer-centric practices.

In conclusion, customer focus is a foundational principle of Total Quality Management (TQM) that underscores the critical importance of understanding and meeting customer needs and expectations. By aligning all aspects of the organization with the customer's perspective, organizations can enhance customer satisfaction, loyalty, and ultimately, their long-term success and competitiveness. Customer focus is not a one-time effort but an ongoing commitment to delivering value to customers.

C. Employee Involvement and Empowerment in Total Quality Management (TQM): Driving Excellence through Engagement

Employee involvement and empowerment are core principles of Total Quality Management (TQM) that emphasize the active participation, commitment, and ownership of all employees in the pursuit of quality and organizational excellence. TQM recognizes that employees are valuable assets who possess the knowledge, insights, and creativity needed to drive continuous improvement and deliver superior products and services. In this section, we will explore the in-depth concepts and practices of employee involvement and empowerment within TQM.

Understanding Employee Involvement and Empowerment in TQM:

1. **Employee Involvement:** This refers to the active participation of employees at all levels of an organization in quality improvement initiatives, decision-making processes, problem-solving, and innovation.

2. **Employee Empowerment:** Empowerment involves granting employees the authority, autonomy, and responsibility to make decisions, take initiative, and contribute to quality and process improvements.

Key Practices for Employee Involvement and Empowerment in TQM:

1. **Team-Based Approaches:** TQM encourages the formation of cross-functional teams or quality circles that work together to identify issues, develop solutions, and implement improvements.

2. **Participative Decision-Making:** Employees are involved in decision-making processes related to quality and process improvements, ensuring that their insights are considered.

3. **Suggestion Systems:** Organizations establish suggestion systems that allow employees to submit ideas for

improvements, which are then reviewed, implemented, and recognized.

4. **Training and Development:** Providing training and development opportunities equips employees with the skills and knowledge needed to contribute effectively to quality initiatives.

5. **Communication and Feedback:** Open and transparent communication channels ensure that employees are informed about quality objectives, progress, and performance. Feedback mechanisms allow employees to express their concerns and ideas.

6. **Recognition and Rewards:** Recognizing and rewarding employees for their contributions to quality improvement fosters motivation and a sense of ownership.

7. **Delegation of Authority:** Empowerment involves delegating authority to employees to make decisions within their areas of expertise, reducing the need for hierarchical approvals.

8. **Continuous Learning:** TQM organizations encourage a culture of continuous learning, where employees are motivated to seek new knowledge and skills to support quality improvement.

Benefits of Employee Involvement and Empowerment in TQM:

1. **Enhanced Problem Solving:** Engaged and empowered employees are better equipped to identify and solve problems at their source, reducing the recurrence of issues.

2. **Higher Morale and Job Satisfaction:** Involvement and empowerment increase employee morale, job satisfaction, and commitment to the organization.

3. **Innovation:** Employees who feel empowered are more likely to innovate and contribute creative solutions to organizational challenges.

4. **Better Quality and Productivity:** Involvement and empowerment contribute to higher quality products and services and improved productivity.

5. **Reduced Turnover:** Organizations with empowered and involved employees often experience lower turnover rates and higher retention of top talent.

6. **Faster Decision-Making:** Decentralized decision-making accelerates problem resolution and response to customer needs.

Challenges in Implementing Employee Involvement and Empowerment:

1. **Cultural Resistance:** Some organizational cultures may resist the shift toward employee involvement and empowerment, requiring strong leadership support to overcome resistance.

2. **Lack of Skills and Training:** Employees may require training to develop the necessary skills for participation and empowerment.

3. **Balancing Authority and Accountability:** Empowerment should be balanced with clear accountability to ensure responsible decision-making.

4. **Communication Barriers:** Ineffective communication can hinder employee involvement and empowerment efforts.

Integrating Employee Involvement and Empowerment into TQM:

To integrate employee involvement and empowerment effectively into TQM, organizations should:

1. **Promote Leadership Support:** Leadership must actively champion and support employee involvement and empowerment initiatives.

2. **Provide Training:** Offer training programs that equip

employees with the skills and knowledge needed for active participation and decision-making.

3. **Establish Feedback Mechanisms:** Implement regular feedback mechanisms to gauge employee satisfaction, identify concerns, and gather improvement suggestions.

4. **Recognize and Reward:** Recognize and reward employees for their contributions to quality improvement, creating a culture of appreciation.

5. **Encourage Learning:** Foster a culture of continuous learning and development to empower employees to take on new challenges and responsibilities.

In conclusion, employee involvement and empowerment are integral to the success of Total Quality Management (TQM). Engaged and empowered employees are essential drivers of continuous improvement, innovation, and the delivery of high-quality products and services. TQM organizations recognize that employees are not just workers but partners in the pursuit of excellence, and they actively involve and empower them to contribute to the organization's quality goals and overall success.

D. Continuous Improvement Methods in Total Quality Management (TQM): Pursuing Perfection

Continuous improvement is at the heart of Total Quality Management (TQM). TQM organizations are committed to the ongoing enhancement of processes, products, and services to deliver ever-higher levels of quality and customer satisfaction. This commitment to continuous improvement is achieved through various systematic methods and approaches. In this section, we will explore in-depth the continuous improvement methods used in TQM.

Key Continuous Improvement Methods in TQM:

1. **Kaizen:** Kaizen is a Japanese term that means "continuous improvement." It involves making small, incremental improvements to processes, products, or services on an ongoing basis. Kaizen emphasizes employee involvement and empowerment, encouraging workers to identify and solve problems as they arise. These improvements accumulate over time, leading to significant enhancements in quality and efficiency.

2. **Six Sigma:** Six Sigma is a data-driven methodology focused on reducing defects and variations in processes. It uses a structured problem-solving approach, commonly referred to as DMAIC (Define, Measure, Analyze, Improve, Control), to

identify and eliminate the root causes of defects. Six Sigma aims to achieve near-perfect quality by minimizing process variations.

3. **Lean:** Lean principles, often associated with Lean Manufacturing, aim to eliminate waste in processes. Waste, in this context, refers to any activity that does not add value from the customer's perspective. Lean tools and techniques, such as Value Stream Mapping and 5S, are used to streamline processes, reduce cycle times, and optimize resource utilization.

4. **PDCA (Plan-Do-Check-Act):** The PDCA cycle, also known as the Deming Cycle or Shewhart Cycle, is a continuous improvement framework. It involves planning (identifying opportunities and setting objectives), doing (implementing changes), checking (measuring and evaluating results), and acting (adjusting processes based on feedback). The PDCA cycle is iterative, with each cycle building on the previous one.

5. **TQM Tools:** TQM organizations use various tools and techniques to support continuous improvement efforts. Some common tools include:

   - **Cause-and-Effect Diagram (Ishikawa or Fishbone Diagram):** Used to identify potential causes of problems.

- **Pareto Analysis:** Helps prioritize issues by identifying the most significant contributors to a problem.

- **Control Charts:** Used to monitor process stability and identify variations.

- **Root Cause Analysis:** A systematic approach to identifying the underlying causes of problems.

- **Benchmarking:** Comparing an organization's performance to industry best practices or competitors to identify areas for improvement.

- **FMEA (Failure Mode and Effects Analysis):** Identifying and mitigating potential failure modes in processes or products.

6. **Continuous Learning and Training:** TQM organizations invest in training and development programs to equip employees with the skills and knowledge needed for continuous improvement. Training may include problem-solving techniques, statistical analysis, and quality tools.

7. **Quality Circles:** Quality circles are small, cross-functional groups of employees who meet regularly to identify and address quality-related issues. They contribute ideas and solutions to improve processes and quality.

8. **Total Productive Maintenance (TPM):** TPM aims to

maximize equipment and machine efficiency by involving operators in maintenance and equipment improvement activities. TPM reduces unplanned downtime and defects.

9. **5 Whys Analysis:** This technique involves asking "why" repeatedly to uncover the root causes of a problem. By addressing the root causes, organizations can prevent problems from recurring.

Benefits of Continuous Improvement in TQM:

1. **Enhanced Quality:** Continuous improvement methods lead to higher product and service quality, resulting in increased customer satisfaction.

2. **Efficiency and Cost Reduction:** Streamlined processes and waste reduction lead to improved efficiency and lower operational costs.

3. **Innovation:** Continuous improvement fosters a culture of innovation, encouraging employees to seek better ways of doing things.

4. **Competitive Advantage:** Organizations that consistently improve their products and processes gain a competitive edge in the market.

5. **Employee Engagement:** Involving employees in improvement initiatives increases their engagement, job

satisfaction, and sense of ownership.

6. **Customer Loyalty:** High-quality products and services generated through continuous improvement efforts result in increased customer loyalty and retention.

Challenges in Implementing Continuous Improvement:

1. **Resistance to Change:** Employees and management may resist changes to established processes and routines.

2. **Resource Constraints:** Continuous improvement efforts may require additional resources, such as time, personnel, and technology.

3. **Lack of Data and Metrics:** Effective continuous improvement relies on data and metrics to identify issues and track progress. Organizations may struggle with data collection and analysis.

4. **Leadership Support:** A lack of leadership commitment and support can hinder the implementation of continuous improvement initiatives.

Integrating Continuous Improvement into TQM:

To effectively integrate continuous improvement into TQM, organizations should:

1. **Cultivate a Culture of Continuous Improvement:** Foster a

culture where continuous improvement is encouraged, recognized, and rewarded.

2. **Provide Training and Support:** Offer training programs and resources to equip employees with the skills and knowledge needed for improvement efforts.

3. **Set Clear Objectives:** Establish clear and measurable improvement objectives aligned with the organization's strategic goals.

4. **Implement Feedback Mechanisms:** Create feedback loops for employees to submit improvement ideas and provide input on existing processes.

5. **Monitor Progress:** Regularly measure and evaluate the results of improvement initiatives and make necessary adjustments.

In conclusion, continuous improvement methods are the lifeblood of Total Quality Management (TQM). TQM organizations are committed to the ongoing pursuit of excellence, using systematic approaches and tools to drive quality, efficiency, and innovation. Continuous improvement is not a one-time effort but a philosophy that permeates all aspects of the organization, ensuring that it remains responsive to customer needs and market dynamics while striving for perfection.

E. Implementing Total Quality Management (TQM) in Organizations: A Path to Excellence

Implementing Total Quality Management (TQM) in organizations is a complex and transformative process that requires commitment, dedication, and a systematic approach. TQM is not just a set of tools or practices; it's a philosophy that permeates an organization's culture, driving a relentless pursuit of quality and excellence. In this section, we will explore in-depth the key steps and considerations involved in implementing TQM in organizations.

Key Steps in Implementing TQM:

1. **Leadership Commitment:** TQM implementation starts with strong leadership commitment. Top management must endorse the TQM philosophy, communicate its importance, and lead by example. Their commitment serves as a catalyst for change and sets the tone for the entire organization.

2. **Formulate a TQM Vision and Strategy:** Organizations should develop a clear vision and strategic plan for TQM implementation. This includes defining quality objectives, identifying target areas for improvement, and setting measurable goals.

3. **Create a Culture of Quality:** TQM requires a cultural shift toward quality and continuous improvement. Organizations

should foster a culture that values quality, empowers employees, encourages innovation, and embraces change.

4. **Employee Involvement:** Actively involve employees at all levels in TQM initiatives. Employees are valuable resources with insights into processes and customer needs. Establish cross-functional teams and quality circles to encourage participation.

5. **Training and Development:** Equip employees with the necessary skills and knowledge for TQM. Provide training in problem-solving techniques, statistical tools, quality principles, and TQM methodologies.

6. **Define Processes and Metrics:** Document and map key processes within the organization. Establish clear metrics and key performance indicators (KPIs) to measure process performance and quality.

7. **Customer Focus:** Understand customer needs and expectations through surveys, feedback mechanisms, and market research. Use this information to drive product and service improvements.

8. **Continuous Improvement:** Implement continuous improvement methodologies like Kaizen, Six Sigma, Lean, and PDCA cycles. Encourage employees to identify and address issues proactively.

9. **Supplier Collaboration:** Collaborate with suppliers to ensure the quality of incoming materials and components. Build strong, mutually beneficial relationships with suppliers.

10. **Communication and Feedback:** Establish effective communication channels to keep employees informed about TQM initiatives and progress. Create feedback mechanisms for employees to express concerns and share improvement ideas.

11. **Recognition and Rewards:** Recognize and reward employees for their contributions to quality improvement. Incentives and recognition programs motivate employees to actively participate in TQM efforts.

12. **Measurement and Analysis:** Implement data collection and analysis processes to monitor progress and identify areas for improvement. Use statistical tools and techniques to make informed decisions.

13. **Benchmarks and Best Practices:** Benchmark against industry best practices and competitors to identify areas for improvement and set performance standards.

14. **Feedback and Adaptation:** Continuously seek feedback from employees and customers and use it to adapt TQM initiatives. TQM is an evolving process that requires ongoing refinement.

Considerations for Successful TQM Implementation:

1. **Customization:** TQM implementation should be tailored to an organization's unique needs, culture, and industry. What works for one organization may not work for another.

2. **Change Management:** TQM involves significant change. Organizations should have a well-defined change management plan to address resistance and ensure smooth transitions.

3. **Resource Allocation:** Implementing TQM may require additional resources, including personnel, technology, and training. Adequate resource allocation is essential for success.

4. **Integration with Strategic Planning:** TQM should be integrated into the organization's strategic planning process. Quality objectives and TQM initiatives should align with the overall strategic goals.

5. **Measurement and Evaluation:** Establish a robust system for measuring and evaluating the impact of TQM initiatives. Regularly review performance against KPIs and adjust strategies as needed.

6. **Customer-Centric Approach:** Keep the customer at the center of TQM efforts. Ensure that customer feedback is not only collected but also acted upon to drive improvements.

7. **Sustainability:** TQM is a long-term commitment. Organizations should be prepared to sustain TQM efforts over time, even after initial improvements are achieved.

8. **Leadership Continuity:** TQM is not tied to a single leader or champion. Organizations should ensure leadership continuity to maintain the momentum of TQM initiatives.

Benefits of TQM Implementation:

1. **Higher Customer Satisfaction:** TQM leads to improved product and service quality, resulting in higher customer satisfaction and loyalty.

2. **Operational Efficiency:** Streamlined processes reduce waste and improve efficiency, leading to cost savings.

3. **Competitive Advantage:** Organizations that excel in quality gain a competitive edge in the market.

4. **Employee Engagement:** TQM fosters a culture of employee involvement and empowerment, leading to higher morale and commitment.

5. **Innovation:** TQM encourages innovation and continuous improvement, driving product and process innovation.

6. **Reduced Defects and Errors:** TQM methodologies like Six Sigma and Lean reduce defects and errors, resulting in higher

quality outcomes.

7. **Long-Term Sustainability:** TQM promotes a culture of excellence and continuous improvement, contributing to long-term organizational sustainability.

In conclusion, implementing Total Quality Management (TQM) in organizations is a strategic journey toward excellence. It involves a cultural shift, strong leadership commitment, employee involvement, systematic methodologies, and a relentless focus on quality and customer satisfaction. TQM is not a one-time project but an ongoing commitment to excellence and continuous improvement, driving organizations to deliver superior products and services and achieve long-term success.

CHAPTER 8

Quality in Service Industries

Quality in service industries is a critical and multifaceted concept that holds immense significance in today's globalized and competitive business landscape. Unlike tangible products, services are intangible and often characterized by direct customer interactions, making quality in service delivery a complex and dynamic endeavor. In this context, the pursuit of quality extends beyond traditional manufacturing processes to encompass customer experiences, responsiveness, reliability, and the ability to consistently meet or exceed customer expectations. This introductory exploration into quality in service industries will delve into the unique challenges, dimensions, and strategies that underpin the quest for service excellence in a diverse range of sectors, from hospitality and healthcare to finance and technology.

A. Service Quality Dimensions: Understanding the Multi-Faceted Nature of Quality in Services

Service quality is a fundamental component of delivering exceptional customer experiences and maintaining a competitive edge in service industries. It encompasses various dimensions that collectively define how well a service meets or exceeds customer expectations. Understanding these dimensions is crucial for organizations aiming to provide high-quality services and gain customer loyalty. In this in-depth exploration, we'll delve into the key service quality dimensions and their significance in service industries.

1. Tangibles:

Tangibles refer to the physical and tangible aspects of the service environment, facilities, equipment, and appearance of personnel. Customers often use tangibles as cues to judge service quality. Clean, well-maintained facilities and professional attire contribute positively to the perception of service quality. In service industries like hospitality and retail, tangibles play a critical role in shaping first impressions.

2. Reliability:

Reliability is the ability of a service provider to deliver consistent and dependable services. Customers expect services to be delivered accurately and on time. Reliability is crucial in industries such as transportation, healthcare, and telecommunications, where any disruption can have a significant impact on customer satisfaction and trust.

3. Responsiveness:

Responsiveness pertains to the willingness and ability of a service provider to assist customers promptly. It involves aspects like attentiveness, quick problem resolution, and a customer-centric approach. Fast response times in industries like customer support, emergency services, and online retail can lead to increased customer satisfaction.

4. Assurance:

Assurance relates to the competence, credibility, and confidence conveyed by service providers. Customers need to feel that they are dealing with knowledgeable and trustworthy individuals or organizations. In industries like finance and healthcare, where expertise is paramount, assurance plays a vital role in building customer trust.

5. Empathy:

Empathy involves understanding and addressing customers' unique needs, concerns, and emotions. Service providers should demonstrate empathy by actively listening, showing compassion, and tailoring services to individual preferences. In healthcare, hospitality, and customer service, empathy can enhance the overall customer experience.

6. Service Recovery:

Service recovery refers to an organization's ability to handle and resolve service failures or customer complaints effectively. No service is flawless, but how an organization handles mistakes or issues can significantly impact customer retention and satisfaction. Industries such as airlines and hotels rely on efficient service recovery mechanisms to retain customer loyalty.

7. Personalization:

Personalization involves tailoring services to meet the specific needs and preferences of individual customers. It goes beyond generic offerings to create a unique and memorable experience. Personalization is vital in industries like e-commerce, where recommendations and customization enhance the customer journey.

8. Accessibility:

Accessibility encompasses how easily customers can access and use services. It considers factors like convenience, availability, and inclusivity. In the digital age, online accessibility is crucial for e-commerce, while physical accessibility is essential in industries like transportation and healthcare.

9. Transparency and Trust:

Transparency and trust are increasingly important dimensions in today's service landscape. Customers expect honesty, openness, and data security from service providers. Trust is especially critical in financial services, data-driven industries, and e-commerce.

10. Cultural Sensitivity:

In a globalized world, cultural sensitivity is essential. It involves understanding and respecting the cultural norms, values, and expectations of diverse customer groups. This dimension is particularly relevant in industries such as hospitality, tourism, and international business.

Significance of Service Quality Dimensions:

- **Competitive Advantage:** Focusing on service quality dimensions can provide a competitive advantage. Organizations that excel in these dimensions differentiate themselves from competitors.

- **Customer Loyalty:** High-quality services lead to increased customer loyalty, repeat business, and positive word-of-mouth referrals.

- **Brand Reputation:** A strong reputation for service quality can enhance a brand's image and credibility.

- **Cost Savings:** Improved service quality can lead to cost savings by reducing service failures, complaints, and the need for extensive service recovery efforts.

- **Employee Satisfaction:** Satisfied employees who understand and embrace service quality dimensions are more likely to deliver exceptional service.

In conclusion, service quality dimensions are essential facets of delivering exceptional service experiences in a wide range of industries. Organizations that recognize and prioritize these dimensions are better equipped to meet customer expectations, build loyalty, and succeed in today's competitive service landscape. Service quality is not a static concept; it evolves with changing customer preferences and market dynamics, making continuous improvement in these dimensions a strategic imperative for businesses.

B. Service Quality Measurement: The Art and Science of Assessing Customer Satisfaction

Measuring service quality is a critical process for service-oriented organizations looking to enhance customer satisfaction, loyalty, and competitiveness. It involves systematically evaluating various aspects of the service experience to understand how well a service meets or exceeds customer expectations. In this in-depth exploration, we'll delve into the intricacies of service quality measurement, examining its methodologies, key dimensions, and the significance it holds for businesses across diverse industries.

Key Dimensions of Service Quality Measurement:

1. **Reliability:**

   - *Definition:* Reliability assesses the consistency and dependability of service delivery. It focuses on whether the service is delivered accurately and as promised.

   - *Measurement Methods:* Metrics like service downtime, error rates, on-time performance, and accuracy of service delivery are used to measure reliability.

   - *Significance:* Reliable services build trust and confidence among customers, leading to repeat business and positive word-of-mouth.

2. **Responsiveness:**

   - *Definition:* Responsiveness evaluates how promptly and effectively a service provider addresses customer needs and inquiries.

   - *Measurement Methods:* Metrics include response times to customer inquiries, complaint resolution time, and the efficiency of handling service requests.

   - *Significance:* Responsive services enhance customer

satisfaction and demonstrate a commitment to customer care.

3. **Assurance:**

- *Definition:* Assurance measures the competence, credibility, and trustworthiness of service personnel and the organization.

- *Measurement Methods:* Surveys, feedback mechanisms, and employee training assessments are used to evaluate assurance.

- *Significance:* Assurance builds customer confidence in the service provider's expertise and integrity.

4. **Empathy:**

- *Definition:* Empathy gauges how well service providers understand and respond to customers' emotional needs and concerns.

- *Measurement Methods:* Customer feedback, surveys, and customer satisfaction ratings are used to assess empathy.

- *Significance:* Empathetic services create strong emotional connections with customers, fostering loyalty and positive experiences.

5. **Tangibles:**

- *Definition:* Tangibles focus on the physical and visual aspects of the service environment, facilities, and personnel appearance.

- *Measurement Methods:* Tangibles are assessed through facility inspections, cleanliness, and personnel appearance evaluations.

- *Significance:* Tangibles influence first impressions and shape customers' perceptions of service quality.

6. **Customer Feedback and Surveys:**

- *Definition:* Gathering direct feedback from customers through surveys, interviews, and feedback forms.

- *Measurement Methods:* Net Promoter Score (NPS), Customer Satisfaction Score (CSAT), and Customer Effort Score (CES) are commonly used metrics.

- *Significance:* Customer feedback provides valuable insights for service improvement and identifies areas of excellence and concern.

7. **Service Recovery:**

- *Definition:* Evaluating how effectively a service provider handles service failures, complaints, and incidents.

- *Measurement Methods:* Tracking the resolution time for complaints, customer satisfaction with service recovery, and the recurrence of service issues.

- *Significance:* Effective service recovery can mitigate the negative impact of service failures and retain customer trust.

8. **Benchmarking:**

- *Definition:* Comparing an organization's service quality performance to industry benchmarks and best practices.

- *Measurement Methods:* Industry-specific benchmarking data and performance metrics.

- *Significance:* Benchmarking helps identify areas for improvement and sets performance standards.

Methods of Service Quality Measurement:

1. **Customer Surveys:**

- Conducting surveys to gather feedback and assess customer satisfaction and perception of service quality.

2. **Mystery Shopping:**

- Employing mystery shoppers who pose as customers to evaluate service quality anonymously.

3. **Service Quality Models:**

- Utilizing established models like SERVQUAL and SERVPERF that provide frameworks for measuring service quality.

4. **Online Reviews and Social Media Monitoring:**

- Analyzing online reviews, comments, and social media mentions to gauge customer sentiment and identify service quality issues.

5. **Employee Feedback:**

- Gathering feedback from employees who interact with customers to gain insights into service quality challenges and opportunities.

6. **Operational Data Analysis:**

- Analyzing operational data, such as service response times, error rates, and service downtime, to assess reliability and responsiveness.

Significance of Service Quality Measurement:

- **Improved Customer Satisfaction:** Measuring service quality helps identify areas for improvement, leading to higher customer satisfaction and loyalty.

- **Competitive Advantage:** Organizations that consistently measure and improve service quality gain a competitive edge in the market.

- **Efficiency and Cost Reduction:** Identifying and addressing service quality issues can lead to cost savings by reducing service failures and customer complaints.

- **Strategic Decision-Making:** Data from service quality measurement informs strategic decisions and resource allocation.

- **Customer Retention:** High service quality leads to increased customer loyalty, reducing customer churn.

In conclusion, service quality measurement is a critical component of delivering exceptional customer experiences and maintaining a competitive edge in service industries. It enables organizations to assess customer satisfaction, identify improvement areas, and make data-driven decisions to enhance service quality continually. In today's customer-centric business landscape, organizations that prioritize service quality measurement are better equipped to meet and exceed customer expectations, driving long-term success.

C. Customer Feedback and Service Improvement: Nurturing Excellence through Valuable Insights

Customer feedback is a cornerstone of service improvement in today's customer-centric business landscape. It provides organizations with valuable insights into customer perceptions, preferences, and expectations, enabling them to enhance their services continually. In this in-depth exploration, we'll delve into the symbiotic relationship between customer feedback and service improvement, examining the methodologies, significance, and best practices for leveraging customer insights effectively.

The Role of Customer Feedback:

Customer feedback serves as a dynamic and invaluable resource for service-oriented organizations. It is a mechanism through which customers communicate their experiences, needs, and concerns, offering a window into the following areas:

1. **Satisfaction Assessment:** Customer feedback measures the level of satisfaction customers derive from a service. It identifies what is working well and where improvements are needed.

2. **Expectation Alignment:** Feedback reveals whether customer expectations align with the service provided. Understanding gaps between expectations and reality is crucial for service improvement.

3. **Issue Identification:** Customers often report problems, errors, or issues they encounter during their interactions with a service. These reports pinpoint areas that require immediate attention.

4. **Opportunity Recognition:** Feedback also highlights opportunities for enhancement, innovation, and differentiation. It can lead to the discovery of unmet needs or underserved segments.

Methods of Gathering Customer Feedback:

1. **Surveys:** Conducting customer satisfaction surveys, Net Promoter Score (NPS) surveys, and Customer Effort Score (CES) surveys to systematically collect structured feedback.

2. **Interviews:** Engaging in one-on-one interviews or focus group discussions with customers to gain in-depth insights into their experiences and preferences.

3. **Online Reviews and Social Media Monitoring:** Analyzing online reviews, comments, and social media mentions to understand public sentiment and identify trends.

4. **Feedback Forms:** Providing feedback forms on websites, mobile apps, or physical locations where customers can submit comments and suggestions.

5. **Customer Support Interactions:** Reviewing interactions with customer support teams, including call logs, chat transcripts, and email correspondence, to identify recurring issues.

Significance of Customer Feedback:

1. **Continuous Improvement:** Customer feedback is a catalyst for continuous service improvement. It helps organizations identify areas for enhancement, prioritize initiatives, and track progress.

2. **Customer-Centricity:** Listening to customers and acting on their feedback demonstrates a commitment to customer-centricity, building trust and loyalty.

3. **Competitive Advantage:** Organizations that actively seek and act upon customer feedback gain a competitive edge by delivering services that align with customer expectations.

4. **Issue Resolution:** Feedback aids in timely issue resolution, preventing customer churn and potential reputation damage.

5. **Innovation:** Insights from customer feedback can spark innovation and new service offerings tailored to customer

needs.

Best Practices for Leveraging Customer Feedback:

1. **Regular Feedback Collection:** Establish a systematic process for collecting customer feedback, whether through surveys, feedback forms, or other means, on a consistent basis.

2. **Multi-Channel Approach:** Utilize multiple channels to gather feedback, recognizing that customers have varying preferences for providing input.

3. **Actionable Insights:** Focus on actionable insights. Prioritize feedback based on its potential to drive significant improvements.

4. **Prompt Response:** Acknowledge and respond to customer feedback promptly, indicating that their input is valued and acted upon.

5. **Closed-Loop Feedback:** Establish closed-loop feedback mechanisms where customers are informed about the actions taken based on their feedback.

6. **Data Analysis:** Employ data analytics to extract meaningful patterns, trends, and correlations from feedback data.

7. **Employee Training:** Train employees on how to collect, handle, and utilize customer feedback effectively.

8. **Integration with Service Design:** Integrate customer feedback into the design and development of services to ensure they align with customer expectations from the outset.

9. **Continuous Monitoring:** Continuously monitor customer feedback to track improvements and address emerging issues.

Challenges in Leveraging Customer Feedback:

1. **Data Overload:** The sheer volume of customer feedback data can be overwhelming. Organizations must have robust data analysis and management processes in place.

2. **Biased Feedback:** Feedback may not always represent the entire customer base, as some customers are more likely to provide feedback than others.

3. **Interpreting Feedback:** It can be challenging to interpret feedback accurately and extract actionable insights from unstructured comments.

4. **Competing Priorities:** Balancing the implementation of customer feedback with other operational priorities can be a challenge.

In conclusion, customer feedback is a potent tool for service improvement that empowers organizations to adapt, innovate, and excel in delivering exceptional customer experiences. When embraced as a strategic asset, customer feedback becomes a catalyst for continuous improvement, customer-centricity, and competitive advantage. By actively listening to their customers and acting on their insights, organizations can cultivate enduring relationships, build brand loyalty, and thrive in an ever-evolving service landscape.

D. Service Quality Standards: The Blueprint for Consistency and Excellence

Service quality standards are the cornerstone of delivering consistent, exceptional service experiences across various industries. They provide organizations with a framework to define, measure, and maintain the quality of services offered to customers. In this comprehensive exploration, we'll delve into the intricacies of service quality standards, their significance, development, and implementation, as well as the benefits they bring to both businesses and customers.

Significance of Service Quality Standards:

1. **Consistency:** Standards ensure that services are delivered consistently, regardless of when, where, or by whom they are provided. This consistency is crucial for building customer trust and loyalty.

2. **Customer Expectations:** Service quality standards align services with customer expectations, helping organizations

meet or exceed these expectations and enhance customer satisfaction.

3. **Benchmarking:** Standards provide a benchmark for organizations to assess their performance, identify areas for improvement, and compare themselves to industry best practices.

4. **Legal and Regulatory Compliance:** In some industries, compliance with service quality standards is a legal requirement, helping organizations avoid legal issues and penalties.

5. **Competitive Advantage:** Organizations that adhere to service quality standards often gain a competitive advantage by demonstrating their commitment to excellence and customer satisfaction.

6. **Continuous Improvement:** Standards encourage organizations to adopt a culture of continuous improvement, leading to ongoing enhancements in service quality.

Development of Service Quality Standards:

1. **Research and Analysis:** Developing service quality standards begins with comprehensive research and analysis of industry best practices, customer expectations, and regulatory requirements.

2. **Defining Metrics:** Organizations must define specific metrics and indicators that will be used to measure service quality. These metrics should be quantifiable and aligned with customer satisfaction.

3. **Setting Targets:** Standards set performance targets based on the defined metrics. These targets should be achievable and reflective of desired service quality levels.

4. **Documenting Processes:** Organizations document the processes and procedures required to meet the established service quality standards. This documentation serves as a guide for employees.

5. **Training and Education:** Employees are trained on the service quality standards, including the metrics, targets, and processes. Training ensures that employees understand and can deliver on these standards.

6. **Continuous Monitoring:** Organizations continually monitor their performance against the standards, collecting data and feedback to assess whether targets are met.

7. **Feedback and Improvement:** Feedback from customers and employees is used to identify areas for improvement. Organizations then take corrective actions to enhance service quality.

Implementation of Service Quality Standards:

1. **Top-Down Commitment:** Successful implementation starts with top management's commitment to service quality. Leaders must endorse the standards and set an example for the entire organization.

2. **Employee Involvement:** Employees at all levels should be involved in the implementation process. They play a critical role in delivering services that meet the established standards.

3. **Communication:** Clear communication of the standards, targets, and expectations is essential. Employees should understand their roles in achieving service quality.

4. **Training and Development:** Employees may require additional training and development to meet the standards. Training programs should be tailored to address specific skill gaps.

5. **Monitoring and Measurement:** Organizations should establish systems for monitoring and measuring performance against the standards. This includes collecting data, conducting regular audits, and soliciting customer feedback.

6. **Recognition and Incentives:** Recognize and reward employees who consistently meet or exceed service quality standards. Incentives can motivate employees to maintain high

levels of service quality.

7. **Continuous Improvement:** Service quality standards are not static. They should be periodically reviewed and updated to reflect changing customer expectations and industry trends.

Types of Service Quality Standards:

1. **Industry-Specific Standards:** Some industries have established sector-specific service quality standards. For example, healthcare has HIPAA (Health Insurance Portability and Accountability Act) standards.

2. **ISO Standards:** The International Organization for Standardization (ISO) has developed various standards related to service quality, such as ISO 9001 for quality management systems.

3. **Regulatory Standards:** In highly regulated industries like finance and healthcare, regulatory bodies often define service quality standards that organizations must adhere to.

Challenges in Implementing Service Quality Standards:

1. **Resistance to Change:** Employees may resist changes required to meet service quality standards, particularly if they perceive them as burdensome.

2. **Resource Allocation:** Implementing standards may require

significant resources, including time, money, and personnel.

3. **Complexity:** Developing and implementing comprehensive service quality standards can be complex, especially for organizations with diverse service offerings.

4. **Measuring Intangibles:** Measuring the quality of intangible services, such as customer support or consulting, can be challenging.

5. **Maintaining Consistency:** Ensuring consistent service quality across multiple locations or teams can be a challenge, requiring ongoing monitoring and support.

In conclusion, service quality standards serve as the foundation for delivering exceptional service experiences and maintaining competitiveness in today's customer-focused marketplace. When developed thoughtfully, communicated effectively, and embraced throughout an organization, these standards enable businesses to consistently meet or exceed customer expectations, drive customer loyalty, and foster a culture of continuous improvement. While the development and implementation of service quality standards require effort and commitment, the long-term benefits for both organizations and customers make them a strategic imperative for service-oriented businesses.

E. Challenges in Ensuring Service Quality: Navigating the Complex Landscape of Customer Satisfaction

Ensuring service quality is a multifaceted endeavor that presents organizations with a range of challenges in today's highly competitive and customer-centric business environment. While delivering exceptional services is paramount, organizations must grapple with numerous obstacles that can impede their efforts to meet or exceed customer expectations. In this comprehensive exploration, we'll delve into the key challenges faced by organizations in ensuring service quality and strategies for addressing these challenges effectively.

1. Understanding Diverse Customer Expectations:

- **Challenge:** Customers have diverse backgrounds, preferences, and expectations. Meeting these varied expectations can be challenging.

- **Strategy:** Conduct comprehensive market research and gather customer feedback to understand diverse customer segments. Tailor services to cater to different customer needs and preferences.

2. Consistency Across Multiple Touchpoints:

- **Challenge:** Maintaining consistent service quality across multiple touchpoints, such as physical locations, online platforms, and customer support channels, is a significant challenge.

- **Strategy:** Implement rigorous training programs, establish standard operating procedures, and leverage technology to ensure consistent service delivery across all touchpoints.

3. Employee Engagement and Training:

- **Challenge:** Ensuring that employees are engaged, motivated, and adequately trained to deliver high-quality services is an ongoing challenge.

- **Strategy:** Invest in employee training and development programs, create a positive work culture that values employees, and recognize and reward outstanding performance.

4. Balancing Cost and Quality:

- **Challenge:** Balancing the cost of delivering high-quality services with the need for profitability can be a delicate equation.

- **Strategy:** Focus on process optimization, cost-efficiency measures, and continuous improvement initiatives to deliver quality services while managing costs effectively.

5. Handling Service Recovery:

- **Challenge:** Service failures and customer complaints are inevitable. Handling these situations effectively to maintain customer trust can be challenging.

- **Strategy:** Establish well-defined service recovery procedures, empower employees to resolve issues promptly, and monitor and learn from service recovery cases.

6. Adapting to Technological Changes:

- **Challenge:** Rapid technological advancements can change customer expectations and disrupt traditional service models.

- **Strategy:** Embrace technology to enhance service quality, implement digital tools for customer engagement, and stay updated on industry trends to adapt proactively.

7. Managing Service Quality in Complex Organizations:

- **Challenge:** Large, complex organizations with multiple departments and functions may struggle to ensure consistent service quality.

- **Strategy:** Implement a robust quality management system, establish cross-functional teams, and foster collaboration across departments to align service quality efforts.

8. Measuring and Monitoring Service Quality:

- **Challenge:** Measuring intangible aspects of service quality and obtaining accurate customer feedback can be difficult.

- **Strategy:** Utilize a combination of metrics, customer feedback, and technology-driven analytics to monitor and measure service quality effectively.

9. Regulatory and Compliance Requirements:

- **Challenge:** Some industries, such as healthcare and finance, are highly regulated, and organizations must navigate complex compliance requirements.

- **Strategy:** Stay informed about industry-specific regulations, invest in compliance training, and establish processes to ensure adherence to legal standards.

10. Cultural and Language Barriers:

- **Challenge:** In global markets, organizations may encounter cultural and language barriers that affect service quality.

- **Strategy:** Foster cultural sensitivity within the organization, provide language training to employees, and adapt services to accommodate diverse cultural norms.

11. Scalability and Growth:

- **Challenge:** Maintaining service quality while scaling and growing the business can be a formidable challenge.

- **Strategy:** Plan for scalability from the outset, leverage technology to automate processes, and invest in a scalable infrastructure that can accommodate growth.

12. Competitive Pressures:

- **Challenge:** Intense competition puts pressure on organizations to innovate and differentiate their services.

- **Strategy:** Focus on innovation, value-added services, and a customer-centric approach to stand out in a competitive landscape.

13. Data Privacy and Security:

- **Challenge:** Protecting customer data and ensuring privacy and security in service delivery is a growing concern.

- **Strategy:** Implement robust data security measures, comply with data protection regulations, and build trust by demonstrating a commitment to data privacy.

14. Sustainability and Environmental Considerations:

- **Challenge:** Incorporating sustainability practices into service delivery while maintaining quality can be complex.

- **Strategy:** Develop sustainable practices, adhere to environmental regulations, and communicate sustainability efforts to customers.

In conclusion, ensuring service quality is an ongoing journey that requires organizations to navigate a complex landscape of challenges. Addressing these challenges effectively involves a combination of strategic planning, employee engagement, customer-centricity, technological innovation, and a commitment to continuous improvement. By embracing these strategies and proactively addressing the challenges, organizations can not only meet but exceed customer expectations, drive customer loyalty, and thrive in today's dynamic and competitive business environment.

CHAPTER 9

Quality Management in Manufacturing

Quality management in manufacturing is the bedrock upon which the success and reputation of manufacturing organizations rest. It is a systematic approach that encompasses all aspects of production, from raw material procurement to final product delivery. In this introductory exploration, we embark on a journey into the world of quality management in manufacturing, highlighting its pivotal role in delivering products that meet or exceed customer expectations while ensuring efficiency, compliance, and continuous improvement.

A. Manufacturing Quality Control: The Pillar of Excellence in Production

Manufacturing quality control (QC) is a critical component of the overall quality management process in manufacturing organizations. It encompasses a set of systematic activities and procedures aimed at ensuring that products meet predefined quality standards and specifications throughout the production process. In this comprehensive exploration, we delve into the intricacies of manufacturing quality control, its significance, methodologies, and the pivotal role it plays in delivering products of superior quality and reliability.

The Significance of Manufacturing Quality Control:

1. **Consistency and Uniformity:** QC processes ensure that products are consistently manufactured to meet established standards, resulting in uniformity and reliability.

2. **Customer Satisfaction:** High-quality products derived from effective QC lead to enhanced customer satisfaction and loyalty, as customers can rely on the consistent performance of products.

3. **Cost Reduction:** Effective QC reduces the likelihood of defects, rework, and waste, ultimately lowering production costs and increasing profitability.

4. **Regulatory Compliance:** Many industries have stringent regulatory requirements, and QC ensures adherence to these standards, avoiding legal and compliance issues.

5. **Competitive Advantage:** Organizations that maintain rigorous QC processes gain a competitive edge by delivering superior products that outperform rivals.

Methodologies of Manufacturing Quality Control:

1. **Incoming Material Inspection:**

   - QC starts at the very beginning of the production

process with the inspection of raw materials, components, or parts. This ensures that only high-quality materials are used in production.

2. **In-Process Inspection:**

- During manufacturing, in-process inspections are conducted at various stages to identify and rectify any deviations from quality standards. This prevents the production of defective products.

3. **Statistical Process Control (SPC):**

- SPC involves the use of statistical techniques to monitor and control production processes. It helps in detecting variations and ensuring processes remain within defined limits.

4. **Sampling and Testing:**

- Samples of products are randomly selected and subjected to rigorous testing to verify their quality against predefined standards. This includes physical, chemical, and performance testing.

5. **Root Cause Analysis:**

- When defects are identified, root cause analysis is performed to determine the underlying causes of the issues. This helps in implementing corrective and preventive actions.

6. **Quality Audits:**

   - Internal and external quality audits are conducted to evaluate the effectiveness of QC processes and ensure compliance with standards.

7. **Documentation and Records:**

   - Maintaining detailed records of QC activities, inspection results, and process parameters is crucial for traceability and continuous improvement.

The Role of QC Personnel:

- Qualified and trained QC personnel play a pivotal role in the success of manufacturing quality control. Their responsibilities include conducting inspections, tests, and audits, as well as documenting and reporting findings.

- QC personnel also collaborate with production teams to identify and resolve quality issues promptly. Their expertise in quality control methodologies is essential for maintaining product quality.

Challenges in Manufacturing Quality Control:

1. **Complexity of Products:** The complexity of modern products

can make QC challenging, as it requires a deep understanding of intricate designs and technologies.

2. **Global Supply Chains:** Managing quality control across global supply chains introduces logistical challenges, including language barriers, time zone differences, and cultural variations.

3. **Rapid Technological Changes:** Keeping up with rapidly evolving technologies and manufacturing processes requires ongoing training and adaptation.

4. **Human Error:** Human error remains a potential source of defects, emphasizing the need for stringent training and process automation.

5. **Regulatory Compliance:** Navigating a web of industry-specific regulations and standards demands meticulous attention to detail.

Benefits of Manufacturing Quality Control:

1. **Customer Trust:** High-quality products foster trust and confidence among customers, leading to brand loyalty.

2. **Operational Efficiency:** Reduced defects and rework enhance operational efficiency and minimize waste.

3. **Cost Savings:** Fewer defects and recalls result in cost savings

in the long run.

4. **Market Reputation:** A strong reputation for product quality can open doors to new markets and opportunities.

5. **Continuous Improvement:** QC drives a culture of continuous improvement, leading to innovations and enhanced processes.

In conclusion, manufacturing quality control is a foundational element of producing high-quality products that meet customer expectations and regulatory requirements. By implementing effective QC processes, organizations can not only deliver exceptional products but also gain a competitive edge, reduce operational costs, and establish a solid foundation for growth and success in the dynamic manufacturing landscape.

B. Lean Manufacturing and Quality: The Symbiotic Relationship

Lean manufacturing is a systematic approach to optimizing production processes, minimizing waste, and maximizing efficiency. When integrated with a robust quality management system, lean principles enhance product quality while reducing costs. In this in-depth exploration, we delve into the intricacies of lean manufacturing and its profound impact on quality, examining methodologies, tools, and the symbiotic relationship between lean principles and quality improvement.

The Essence of Lean Manufacturing:

Lean manufacturing, often referred to as simply "lean," originated from the Toyota Production System (TPS) in Japan. It is grounded in principles aimed at eliminating non-value-added activities, reducing waste, and streamlining processes. Key lean principles include:

1. **Value:** Identifying what customers perceive as value and aligning all activities to deliver that value while eliminating waste.

2. **Value Stream:** Analyzing the entire value stream, from raw materials to end customers, to identify and remove inefficiencies.

3. **Flow:** Ensuring smooth, uninterrupted flow of work, materials, and information throughout the production process.

4. **Pull:** Aligning production with actual customer demand to minimize overproduction and reduce inventory.

5. **Perfection:** Pursuing continuous improvement through the elimination of waste and the pursuit of perfection.

Lean Tools and Techniques:

1. **5S:** The 5S methodology (Sort, Set in order, Shine, Standardize, Sustain) creates an organized, efficient

workplace that promotes quality and safety.

2. **Kaizen:** Kaizen, or continuous improvement, encourages small, incremental changes in processes to drive improvements over time.

3. **Kanban:** Kanban systems use visual cues to manage and control inventory, ensuring that materials are replenished only when needed.

4. **Poka-Yoke:** Poka-yoke, or mistake-proofing, involves designing processes or devices to prevent errors and defects.

5. **JIT (Just-in-Time):** JIT aims to reduce inventory by delivering materials or components precisely when needed in the production process.

The Synergy with Quality:

1. **Reduction of Defects:** Lean manufacturing emphasizes process stability and error prevention, leading to a significant reduction in defects and errors.

2. **Enhanced Quality Assurance:** Lean principles incorporate built-in quality checks at every stage of production, ensuring that defects are identified and corrected early.

3. **Continuous Improvement:** The culture of continuous improvement within lean manufacturing promotes the

identification and elimination of root causes of defects, contributing to long-term quality enhancement.

4. **Customer Focus:** Lean practices center on delivering value to customers, aligning closely with quality management's customer-centric approach.

5. **Standardization:** Lean encourages standardized work processes, reducing variability and increasing product consistency.

6. **Waste Reduction:** Waste elimination in lean not only reduces costs but also enhances product quality by eliminating non-value-added activities that can introduce defects.

Challenges in Implementing Lean for Quality Improvement:

1. **Resistance to Change:** Employees may resist changes in processes, requiring effective change management strategies.

2. **Resource Allocation:** Implementing lean practices may necessitate initial investments in training, equipment, and process redesign.

3. **Complex Processes:** In some cases, adapting lean principles to complex manufacturing processes can be challenging.

4. **Measuring Quality:** Defining and measuring quality in a way

that aligns with lean principles can be a nuanced task.

Benefits of Lean Manufacturing for Quality:

1. **Cost Reduction:** By reducing waste and defects, lean practices lead to cost savings over time.

2. **Improved Efficiency:** Lean streamlines processes, improving production efficiency and reducing lead times.

3. **Higher Productivity:** Eliminating non-value-added activities frees up resources for more productive tasks.

4. **Enhanced Customer Satisfaction:** Consistently delivering quality products on time leads to higher customer satisfaction.

5. **Competitive Advantage:** Organizations that embrace lean manufacturing gain a competitive edge by producing high-quality products efficiently.

In conclusion, lean manufacturing and quality are intertwined concepts that, when harmoniously integrated, result in enhanced product quality, reduced costs, and improved customer satisfaction. Lean principles not only reduce waste and inefficiencies but also cultivate a culture of continuous improvement, where quality is not just a goal but a way of doing business. The synergy between lean manufacturing and quality management represents a formidable strategy for organizations seeking to thrive in today's competitive manufacturing landscape.

C. Six Sigma in Manufacturing: Achieving Perfection in Production

Six Sigma is a data-driven methodology and philosophy that strives for continuous process improvement and defect reduction. It has been widely adopted in manufacturing to enhance product quality, reduce defects, and increase operational efficiency. In this comprehensive exploration, we delve into the world of Six Sigma in manufacturing, examining its principles, methodologies, tools, and the profound impact it has on quality and productivity.

The Essence of Six Sigma:

Six Sigma is built upon the following core principles:

1. **Customer Focus:** Identifying and understanding customer needs and expectations are paramount. Six Sigma aims to deliver products that consistently meet or exceed customer requirements.

2. **Data-Driven Decision-Making:** Six Sigma relies on data and statistical analysis to make informed decisions and drive process improvements.

3. **Process Excellence:** The methodology centers on achieving process excellence by reducing variation and minimizing defects.

4. **Continuous Improvement:** Six Sigma embraces the

philosophy of continuous improvement, seeking incremental enhancements in processes and products.

The DMAIC Framework:

The DMAIC (Define, Measure, Analyze, Improve, Control) framework is a structured approach used in Six Sigma projects:

1. **Define:** Define the problem, project goals, and customer requirements. Establish the scope and boundaries of the project.

2. **Measure:** Measure and collect data on the current process to assess its performance and identify sources of variation.

3. **Analyze:** Analyze the data to identify the root causes of defects and process inefficiencies. Use statistical tools to pinpoint areas for improvement.

4. **Improve:** Develop and implement solutions to address the identified issues. These solutions are aimed at reducing defects and improving process performance.

5. **Control:** Implement control measures to sustain the improvements achieved. Monitor the process to ensure it continues to meet desired quality standards.

Key Six Sigma Tools and Methodologies:

1. **Statistical Process Control (SPC):** SPC involves monitoring

and controlling a process to ensure it remains within predefined limits. Control charts and data analysis are key components.

2. **Design of Experiments (DOE):** DOE is used to systematically vary process factors to identify which factors influence product quality and how they interact.

3. **Failure Mode and Effects Analysis (FMEA):** FMEA is a structured approach for identifying potential failure modes in a process and assessing their impact and likelihood.

4. **Root Cause Analysis:** Techniques like the 5 Whys and Fishbone (Ishikawa) diagram are employed to determine the underlying causes of defects.

5. **Regression Analysis:** Regression analysis is used to identify relationships between variables and to predict the impact of changes on the process.

The Role of Green Belts and Black Belts:

- In Six Sigma, individuals are often trained and certified as Green Belts and Black Belts. They play key roles in leading and executing Six Sigma projects.

- Green Belts typically work on smaller projects within their functional areas, while Black Belts lead larger, more complex projects and mentor Green Belts.

Benefits of Six Sigma in Manufacturing:

1. **Defect Reduction:** Six Sigma leads to a significant reduction in defects, resulting in higher product quality and customer satisfaction.

2. **Cost Savings:** Reduced defects and waste translate into cost savings, including decreased scrap, rework, and warranty expenses.

3. **Improved Efficiency:** Six Sigma optimizes processes, leading to increased operational efficiency and reduced lead times.

4. **Consistency:** Manufacturing processes become more consistent and predictable, contributing to better quality control.

5. **Customer Loyalty:** Consistently delivering high-quality products fosters customer loyalty and strengthens brand reputation.

Challenges in Implementing Six Sigma in Manufacturing:

1. **Resistance to Change:** Employees may resist changes in processes or feel overwhelmed by the rigorous data-driven approach.

2. **Data Availability:** Obtaining accurate and relevant data can

be a challenge, particularly in organizations with legacy systems.

3. **Resource Allocation:** Implementing Six Sigma requires dedicated resources for training, project execution, and data analysis.

4. **Integration with Culture:** Embedding Six Sigma principles into the organizational culture may take time and effort.

Conclusion:

Six Sigma in manufacturing is a powerful methodology that not only enhances product quality but also contributes to overall operational excellence. It combines data-driven decision-making with a structured problem-solving approach to drive continuous improvement and defect reduction. By embracing Six Sigma principles and methodologies, manufacturing organizations can achieve higher levels of quality, efficiency, and customer satisfaction while remaining competitive in today's global marketplace.

D. Quality Management in the Automotive Industry: Driving Excellence and Innovation

The automotive industry is synonymous with precision, safety, and innovation. Ensuring that vehicles meet stringent quality standards is not only a business imperative but also a matter of public safety. In this comprehensive exploration, we dive into the world of quality management in the automotive industry, examining its principles, practices, challenges, and the crucial role it plays in producing safe and reliable vehicles.

The Significance of Quality in the Automotive Industry:

1. **Safety:** Quality is paramount in the automotive industry to ensure the safety of drivers, passengers, and pedestrians. Defects or failures in vehicles can have catastrophic consequences.

2. **Compliance:** Strict regulatory standards and government regulations demand that vehicles meet specific quality and safety criteria before they can be sold to the public.

3. **Customer Expectations:** Automotive consumers expect high-quality, reliable, and technologically advanced vehicles. Meeting these expectations is essential for brand loyalty and reputation.

4. **Competitive Advantage:** Quality differentiation can be a significant competitive advantage, allowing automakers to command higher prices and gain market share.

5. **Reduced Warranty Costs:** High-quality vehicles are less likely to experience warranty claims and recalls, reducing warranty-related expenses for manufacturers.

Quality Management Systems (QMS) in the Automotive Industry:

1. **ISO/TS 16949:** This quality management system standard is specifically designed for the automotive industry. It emphasizes process efficiency, defect prevention, and continuous improvement.

2. **ISO 9001:** While not exclusive to the automotive sector, ISO 9001 provides a general framework for quality management. Many automotive companies also adhere to this standard.

Key Quality Management Practices in the Automotive Industry:

1. **Advanced Product Quality Planning (APQP):** APQP is a structured process that guides manufacturers in developing and introducing new products while ensuring that quality is integrated from the outset.

2. **Failure Mode and Effects Analysis (FMEA):** FMEA is used to identify potential failure modes in a product or process and assess their impact and likelihood.

3. **Statistical Process Control (SPC):** SPC involves monitoring and controlling production processes to ensure they remain within predefined quality limits.

4. **Six Sigma:** Six Sigma methodologies are used extensively in

the automotive industry to reduce defects and improve processes.

Quality Control in Manufacturing:

1. **Incoming Inspection:** Components and materials are rigorously inspected upon arrival to ensure they meet specifications.

2. **In-Process Inspection:** Throughout the manufacturing process, inspections are conducted to identify defects and deviations from standards.

3. **End-of-Line Testing:** Vehicles undergo comprehensive testing before leaving the assembly line to ensure they meet safety and quality requirements.

4. **Quality Audits:** Internal and external audits are performed to evaluate adherence to quality standards and regulatory compliance.

Challenges in Quality Management in the Automotive Industry:

1. **Complex Supply Chain:** Managing the quality of components and materials from a global supply chain can be challenging.

2. **Technology Integration:** Rapid technological advancements

require automotive companies to adapt and integrate new technologies seamlessly.

3. **Recalls and Product Liability:** The automotive industry faces the risk of product recalls and legal liability for defects or safety-related issues.

4. **Regulatory Changes:** Frequent changes in safety and environmental regulations require continuous adaptation and compliance efforts.

5. **Global Competition:** Intense global competition necessitates continuous quality improvements to maintain market share.

Benefits of Effective Quality Management in the Automotive Industry:

1. **Enhanced Safety:** High-quality vehicles contribute to road safety by reducing the likelihood of accidents caused by mechanical failures.

2. **Customer Loyalty:** Quality vehicles lead to satisfied customers who are more likely to remain loyal to a brand.

3. **Reduced Warranty Costs:** Fewer defects translate into lower warranty-related expenses for manufacturers.

4. **Improved Efficiency:** Efficient manufacturing processes result in cost savings and reduced lead times.

5. **Competitive Advantage:** Maintaining a reputation for producing high-quality vehicles sets companies apart in a crowded market.

Conclusion:

Quality management in the automotive industry is not an option but a necessity. It underpins safety, compliance, customer satisfaction, and competitiveness. In an era of rapid technological advancement and global competition, automotive manufacturers that prioritize and excel in quality management are poised to lead the industry, produce safer vehicles, and innovate for a sustainable and connected future on the roads.

E. Quality Management in the Pharmaceutical Industry: Ensuring Safety and Efficacy

The pharmaceutical industry operates at the intersection of science, medicine, and business, and its products directly impact human health and well-being. Quality management in this sector is of paramount importance, as it involves ensuring the safety, efficacy, and reliability of medications and healthcare products. In this comprehensive exploration, we delve into the intricate world of quality management in the pharmaceutical industry, examining its principles, regulatory landscape, challenges, and the pivotal role it plays in safeguarding public health.

The Significance of Quality in the Pharmaceutical Industry:

1. **Patient Safety:** Quality in pharmaceuticals directly affects patient safety. Any lapse in quality can have life-threatening consequences.

2. **Regulatory Compliance:** The pharmaceutical industry is highly regulated globally to ensure product quality, safety, and efficacy.

3. **Public Trust:** Maintaining public trust is essential. High-quality pharmaceuticals contribute to a positive industry reputation and patient confidence.

4. **Innovation and Research:** Quality control is crucial for research and development, as it ensures reliable data and results in drug discovery.

5. **Market Access:** Quality is a prerequisite for market access and international trade, as regulatory authorities demand evidence of product quality.

Quality Management Systems (QMS) in the Pharmaceutical Industry:

1. **Current Good Manufacturing Practices (cGMP):** cGMP regulations outline the minimum requirements for the methods, facilities, and controls used in manufacturing,

processing, and packaging of pharmaceutical products.

2. **International Council for Harmonisation of Technical Requirements for Pharmaceuticals for Human Use (ICH):** ICH provides global guidelines for pharmaceutical quality, with a focus on harmonizing regulatory requirements.

3. **ISO 9001:** Some pharmaceutical companies adopt ISO 9001 as a foundation for their QMS to ensure consistent quality across all processes.

Key Quality Management Practices in the Pharmaceutical Industry:

1. **Quality by Design (QbD):** QbD is an approach that emphasizes the proactive design of quality into pharmaceutical products, processes, and systems.

2. **Risk-Based Approach:** Quality risk management is integral to pharmaceutical quality systems, helping to identify, assess, and control risks.

3. **Validation and Qualification:** Processes, equipment, and computer systems must be validated to ensure they perform as intended.

4. **Change Control:** Strict change control procedures are in place to assess and manage any changes that may impact product quality.

Quality Control and Assurance in Pharmaceutical Manufacturing:

1. **Analytical Testing:** Rigorous testing and analysis are performed to verify the identity, purity, and potency of pharmaceutical products.

2. **Stability Testing:** Products undergo stability testing to determine their shelf life and how they may change over time.

3. **Batch Release:** Each batch of pharmaceutical products must be approved for release by a qualified person in accordance with regulatory requirements.

4. **Documentation and Recordkeeping:** Comprehensive documentation is maintained to provide evidence of quality compliance.

Challenges in Quality Management in the Pharmaceutical Industry:

1. **Stringent Regulations:** The pharmaceutical industry is subject to a complex web of regulations that require constant monitoring and compliance.

2. **Global Supply Chain:** Managing the quality of components and materials from a global supply chain can be challenging.

3. **Counterfeit Drugs:** The pharmaceutical industry faces the

challenge of combatting counterfeit drugs that pose serious health risks.

4. **Technological Advancements:** The rapid advancement of technology necessitates continuous adaptation and validation of processes.

5. **Data Integrity:** Ensuring the integrity and authenticity of data is a priority due to its crucial role in quality management.

Benefits of Effective Quality Management in the Pharmaceutical Industry:

1. **Patient Safety:** Effective quality management ensures the safety and efficacy of medications, minimizing health risks.

2. **Compliance:** Regulatory compliance allows pharmaceutical companies to maintain market access and international trade.

3. **Efficiency:** Efficient manufacturing and quality processes reduce operational costs and time-to-market.

4. **Innovation:** Quality control and assurance foster innovation by providing reliable data and results.

5. **Reputation:** Maintaining a reputation for producing high-quality pharmaceuticals is essential for long-term success.

Conclusion:

Quality management in the pharmaceutical industry is a matter of life and death. It is a multifaceted and highly regulated endeavor aimed at ensuring that medications and healthcare products are safe, effective, and reliable. By adhering to stringent quality standards, embracing continuous improvement, and navigating complex regulatory landscapes, pharmaceutical companies fulfill their mission to provide life-saving and life-enhancing solutions to people around the world while safeguarding public health.

CHAPTER 10

Regulatory Compliance and Quality

In today's highly regulated business landscape, the nexus between regulatory compliance and quality has become central to the success and integrity of organizations across various industries. The journey to deliver products and services of impeccable quality while adhering to a labyrinth of legal requirements is a complex and critical undertaking. In this introductory exploration, we embark on a voyage into the world where regulatory compliance and quality converge, examining the essential principles, challenges, and the pivotal role they play in ensuring excellence within legal frameworks.

A. Quality Regulations: FDA, ISO, and GMP - Pillars of Quality Assurance

Quality regulations serve as the bedrock upon which industries, particularly pharmaceuticals, food, and manufacturing, build their quality management systems. Three prominent regulatory bodies that have shaped the landscape of quality assurance are the U.S. Food and Drug Administration (FDA), the International Organization for Standardization (ISO), and Good Manufacturing Practices (GMP). In this comprehensive exploration, we delve into the intricacies of these quality regulations, their significance, and their impact on ensuring product safety, efficacy, and compliance.

FDA (U.S. Food and Drug Administration):

Significance:

- The FDA is a federal agency of the U.S. Department of Health and Human Services responsible for protecting public health by ensuring the safety, efficacy, and security of human and veterinary drugs, vaccines, biological products, medical devices, blood transfusions, radiation-emitting devices, and veterinary products.

Key Regulatory Functions:

1. **Drug Approval:** The FDA reviews and approves new drugs, generic drugs, and biosimilar products, ensuring their safety and efficacy before they reach the market.

2. **Medical Device Regulation:** It regulates the design, manufacturing, and marketing of medical devices, ensuring they meet quality and safety standards.

3. **Food Safety:** The FDA oversees food safety, including labeling, additives, and contaminants, to protect consumers from unsafe products.

4. **Biological Products:** It regulates vaccines, blood and blood

products, allergenic products, and cell, tissue, and gene therapies.

5. **Inspections and Compliance:** The FDA conducts inspections of manufacturing facilities to ensure compliance with quality standards and regulatory requirements.

Challenges:

- Adhering to FDA regulations requires rigorous testing, documentation, and compliance efforts, which can be resource-intensive for organizations.

ISO (International Organization for Standardization):

Significance:

- ISO is a globally recognized body that develops and publishes international standards for products, services, and systems to ensure quality, safety, and efficiency.

Key Standards:

1. **ISO 9001 (Quality Management System):** This standard sets the criteria for a quality management system that helps organizations consistently meet customer and regulatory requirements.

2. **ISO 14001 (Environmental Management):** It focuses on environmental management systems, helping organizations

reduce their environmental impact.

3. **ISO 45001 (Occupational Health and Safety Management):** This standard ensures the health and safety of employees in the workplace.

Benefits:

- ISO standards provide a framework for organizations to enhance quality, improve efficiency, and demonstrate commitment to quality management.

Challenges:

- Implementing ISO standards often requires a cultural shift and significant organizational change, which can be met with resistance.

GMP (Good Manufacturing Practices):

Significance:

- GMP is a set of regulations enforced by the FDA, among other regulatory agencies worldwide, to ensure the quality and safety of pharmaceuticals and medical devices.

Key Regulatory Functions:

1. **Quality Assurance:** GMP establishes quality control systems to ensure the consistent production of safe and effective

products.

2. **Documentation and Records:** Thorough documentation is essential to trace product quality and adherence to standards.

3. **Personnel Training:** GMP mandates that personnel are adequately trained to perform their duties.

4. **Facility and Equipment:** It outlines requirements for facilities and equipment used in manufacturing.

Benefits:

- GMP ensures that pharmaceutical and medical device products are manufactured, tested, and controlled according to quality standards, reducing the risk of contamination and defects.

Challenges:

- Complying with GMP can be complex and resource-intensive, often requiring significant investments in infrastructure and training.

The Interplay of Regulations:

- Organizations operating within regulated industries must navigate the interplay between FDA, ISO, GMP, and other relevant regulations to ensure compliance while maintaining high-quality standards.

Conclusion:

Quality regulations, whether enforced by the FDA, guided by ISO, or embodied in GMP, are essential to safeguarding public health, ensuring product quality, and fostering international trade. These regulations establish a framework for organizations to build robust quality management systems, reducing the risk of safety breaches, defects, and recalls. By adhering to and embracing the principles of these regulations, organizations demonstrate their commitment to excellence, compliance, and the well-being of consumers and patients around the world.

B. Compliance Auditing: Ensuring Adherence to Regulatory Standards

Compliance auditing is a critical process for organizations in various industries to ensure that they are operating within the boundaries of relevant laws, regulations, and standards. This systematic examination of an organization's operations, policies, and procedures aims to verify compliance, identify areas of non-compliance, and mitigate potential risks. In this in-depth exploration, we delve into the world of compliance auditing, its methodologies, challenges, and the pivotal role it plays in maintaining legal and ethical integrity within organizations.

The Significance of Compliance Auditing:

1. **Legal Obligations:** Organizations are legally bound to adhere to industry-specific regulations and standards. Non-compliance can lead to legal consequences, fines, and reputational damage.

2. **Risk Mitigation:** Identifying and rectifying non-compliance issues through audits helps organizations proactively manage risks, preventing potential liabilities and operational disruptions.

3. **Enhanced Reputation:** Demonstrating commitment to regulatory compliance enhances an organization's reputation and fosters trust among stakeholders, including customers, investors, and partners.

4. **Operational Efficiency:** Compliance audits often uncover inefficiencies, which, when addressed, can lead to cost savings and improved processes.

Key Components of Compliance Auditing:

1. **Audit Planning:** Defining audit objectives, scope, and criteria. Identifying key risk areas and selecting appropriate audit methodologies.

2. **Document Review:** Examining relevant documents, policies, procedures, and records to assess compliance.

3. **Fieldwork:** Conducting interviews, observations, and sample testing to gather evidence of compliance or non-compliance.

4. **Data Analysis:** Utilizing data analytics tools to identify patterns and anomalies in large datasets, aiding in the detection of irregularities.

5. **Reporting:** Documenting findings, including areas of compliance, non-compliance, and recommendations for remediation. Reports should be clear, concise, and actionable.

6. **Follow-Up:** Ensuring that corrective actions are taken to address identified non-compliance issues. Follow-up audits may be conducted to verify remediation efforts.

Types of Compliance Audits:

1. **Financial Compliance Audits:** Ensuring compliance with financial reporting standards, tax regulations, and internal financial controls.

2. **Operational Compliance Audits:** Focusing on adherence to operational procedures, quality standards, and industry-specific regulations.

3. **Information Security Compliance Audits:** Assessing compliance with data protection laws and security standards to safeguard sensitive information.

4. **Environmental Compliance Audits:** Ensuring adherence to environmental laws and regulations related to emissions, waste disposal, and sustainability.

5. **Regulatory Compliance Audits:** Verifying compliance with industry-specific regulations, such as FDA requirements in pharmaceuticals or HIPAA in healthcare.

Challenges in Compliance Auditing:

1. **Complex Regulations:** Regulations are often intricate and subject to change, making it challenging to stay updated and interpret compliance requirements correctly.

2. **Data Volume and Complexity:** The volume and complexity of data in modern organizations can be overwhelming, requiring advanced analytics tools and expertise.

3. **Resource Allocation:** Conducting audits demands resources in terms of time, personnel, and technology, which can strain budgets and manpower.

4. **Audit Independence:** Maintaining the independence and objectivity of auditors is crucial to ensuring unbiased assessments.

5. **Global Operations:** Multinational organizations must navigate a complex web of international regulations, requiring specialized expertise.

Benefits of Effective Compliance Auditing:

1. **Risk Mitigation:** Identifying non-compliance issues early allows organizations to take corrective action, reducing legal and financial risks.

2. **Operational Improvement:** Compliance audits often uncover inefficiencies and opportunities for process improvement, enhancing overall operations.

3. **Legal Protection:** Demonstrating diligent efforts to comply with regulations can serve as legal protection in case of regulatory investigations.

4. **Enhanced Reputation:** A commitment to compliance bolsters an organization's reputation, fostering trust among stakeholders.

5. **Strategic Insights:** Compliance audits can provide valuable insights into an organization's strengths, weaknesses, and opportunities for growth.

Conclusion:

Compliance auditing is an indispensable practice that ensures organizations operate within the boundaries of applicable laws, regulations, and standards. It serves as a proactive risk management tool, allowing organizations to identify and rectify non-compliance issues before they escalate into legal or operational crises. By conducting thorough and systematic audits, organizations can maintain legal and ethical integrity, safeguard their reputation, and build trust with stakeholders in an increasingly regulated business environment.

C. Quality and Regulatory Reporting: Navigating the Compliance Landscape

Quality and regulatory reporting are integral components of compliance in various industries, particularly those subject to stringent regulations such as healthcare, pharmaceuticals, finance, and manufacturing. These reporting processes involve documenting and communicating an organization's adherence to quality standards, regulations, and legal requirements. In this comprehensive exploration, we delve into the world of quality and regulatory reporting, examining its significance, challenges, methodologies, and the pivotal role it plays in ensuring legal and ethical integrity within organizations.

The Significance of Quality and Regulatory Reporting:

1. **Legal Compliance:** Quality and regulatory reporting is a legal requirement in many industries. It ensures that organizations adhere to relevant laws, regulations, and industry standards.

2. **Transparency:** Reporting fosters transparency by providing stakeholders, including regulators, investors, and the public,

with a clear view of an organization's compliance efforts.

3. **Risk Mitigation:** Timely and accurate reporting helps identify and mitigate compliance risks, reducing the likelihood of legal actions, fines, or reputational damage.

4. **Operational Efficiency:** Reporting can lead to process improvements, cost savings, and enhanced operational efficiency as organizations identify areas for optimization.

Key Components of Quality and Regulatory Reporting:

1. **Data Collection:** Gathering relevant data from various sources within the organization, including documentation, records, and systems.

2. **Data Analysis:** Analyzing the collected data to assess compliance with regulations, quality standards, and internal policies.

3. **Documentation:** Preparing detailed reports that document compliance efforts, findings, and any areas of non-compliance.

4. **Communication:** Sharing reports with internal stakeholders, such as senior management and compliance officers, as well as external parties, such as regulators and auditors.

5. **Continuous Monitoring:** Establishing processes for ongoing

monitoring and reporting to ensure sustained compliance.

Types of Quality and Regulatory Reporting:

1. **Financial Reporting:** Reporting on an organization's financial performance, including income statements, balance sheets, and cash flow statements, in compliance with accounting standards like GAAP or IFRS.

2. **Quality Assurance and Control Reporting:** Documenting adherence to quality standards, such as ISO, GMP, or industry-specific regulations, to ensure the quality of products and services.

3. **Environmental and Sustainability Reporting:** Reporting on an organization's environmental impact, carbon footprint, and sustainability efforts in compliance with environmental regulations and industry initiatives.

4. **Regulatory Reporting:** Compiling and submitting data and reports to regulatory authorities in accordance with specific regulations, such as FDA submissions in healthcare or financial reporting to regulatory bodies like the SEC.

5. **Internal Audit Reporting:** Reporting on the findings and recommendations of internal audits to assess compliance with internal policies and procedures.

Challenges in Quality and Regulatory Reporting:

1. **Data Management:** Gathering, managing, and analyzing large volumes of data can be complex and resource-intensive.

2. **Changing Regulations:** Regulatory requirements often change, requiring organizations to stay updated and adapt their reporting processes accordingly.

3. **Data Accuracy:** Ensuring the accuracy and reliability of data is crucial to avoid compliance risks.

4. **Interoperability:** Integrating data from disparate systems and sources can be challenging, leading to data silos and reporting inefficiencies.

5. **Timeliness:** Meeting reporting deadlines, especially for regulatory submissions, can be demanding.

Benefits of Effective Quality and Regulatory Reporting:

1. **Compliance Assurance:** Reporting verifies an organization's compliance with legal and regulatory requirements, reducing the risk of non-compliance.

2. **Risk Reduction:** Timely reporting allows organizations to identify and address compliance risks before they escalate.

3. **Transparency:** Reporting promotes transparency and accountability, building trust with stakeholders.

4. **Operational Improvement:** Identifying areas for improvement through reporting can lead to enhanced operational efficiency.

5. **Strategic Decision-Making:** Quality and regulatory reporting provide data-driven insights for strategic decision-making.

Conclusion:

Quality and regulatory reporting are vital components of compliance, legal integrity, and risk management in today's complex regulatory landscape. These processes enable organizations to demonstrate their commitment to compliance, transparency, and accountability. By navigating the challenges and embracing effective reporting methodologies, organizations can not only meet legal requirements but also enhance their operational efficiency, reputation, and ability to make informed strategic decisions in an increasingly regulated business environment.

D. Case Studies in Regulatory Compliance: Learning from Real-World Examples

Case studies in regulatory compliance offer valuable insights into the challenges and successes organizations face when navigating complex regulatory landscapes. These real-world examples provide practical lessons on how to achieve and maintain compliance with various laws, standards, and industry regulations. In this in-depth exploration, we examine several case studies that illustrate the significance of regulatory compliance, the consequences of non-compliance, and the strategies organizations employ to ensure adherence to legal and ethical standards.

1. Volkswagen's Emissions Scandal (2015):

Background: Volkswagen (VW) faced a major compliance crisis when it was revealed that the company had manipulated emissions tests for its diesel vehicles. The scandal involved installing software that reduced emissions during tests but exceeded permissible levels during normal driving.

Consequences: VW faced severe financial penalties, a damaged reputation, and legal repercussions. Top executives resigned, and the company had to recall millions of vehicles to rectify the issue.

Lessons Learned: This case underscores the importance of transparency, honesty, and adherence to environmental regulations. It demonstrates that even large organizations can face significant consequences for non-compliance, including financial and reputational damage.

2. Equifax Data Breach (2017):

Background: Equifax, a credit reporting company, suffered a massive data breach that exposed the personal information of millions of consumers. The breach occurred due to a vulnerability in the company's website software.

Consequences: Equifax faced legal and regulatory investigations, lawsuits, and a loss of trust from consumers. The breach highlighted the importance of data security and regulatory compliance, such as the handling of sensitive customer information.

Lessons Learned: Organizations must prioritize cybersecurity and comply with data protection regulations. Data breaches can have far-reaching consequences, including financial and legal liabilities.

3. Wells Fargo's Unauthorized Accounts Scandal (2016):

Background: Wells Fargo faced a compliance crisis when it was revealed that employees had opened millions of unauthorized accounts to meet aggressive sales targets. This unethical behavior violated banking regulations.

Consequences: Wells Fargo faced regulatory fines, legal actions, and reputational damage. The scandal led to the resignation of top executives and changes in corporate governance.

Lessons Learned: This case emphasizes the need for a strong ethical culture and compliance with financial regulations. It also underscores the importance of effective internal controls and accountability.

4. Theranos and Elizabeth Holmes (2016):

Background: Theranos, a health technology company, claimed to have developed a revolutionary blood-testing technology. However, investigations revealed that the company misled investors and patients about the accuracy and capabilities of its technology.

Consequences: The company faced legal actions, regulatory scrutiny, and the downfall of its founder, Elizabeth Holmes. The case highlights the consequences of fraud and misrepresentation in healthcare.

Lessons Learned: Compliance with healthcare regulations and truthful representation of product capabilities are essential. The case underscores the importance of ethical conduct and transparency in healthcare innovation.

5. Boeing 737 MAX Crashes (2018-2019):

Background: Two fatal crashes involving Boeing's 737 MAX aircraft raised questions about the aircraft's safety and the certification process. Regulatory scrutiny focused on issues related to the aircraft's automated flight control system.

Consequences: Boeing faced regulatory investigations, lawsuits, financial losses, and a damaged reputation. The crashes led to a global grounding of the 737 MAX fleet.

Lessons Learned: Regulatory agencies play a critical role in ensuring the safety of products and services. This case emphasizes the importance of robust regulatory oversight, transparency, and accountability in the aviation industry.

Conclusion:

Case studies in regulatory compliance serve as cautionary tales and sources of valuable lessons for organizations across industries. They highlight the significance of compliance with laws, regulations, and ethical standards, as well as the consequences of non-compliance. By studying these cases, organizations can gain insights into best practices, risk mitigation strategies, and the importance of fostering a culture of compliance and integrity within their operations.

CHAPTER 11

Advanced Topics in Quality Management

As the world of business and industry evolves at an unprecedented pace, the realm of quality management continually adapts and expands to meet new challenges and opportunities. Advanced topics in quality management represent the cutting edge of knowledge and practice, addressing emerging trends, technologies, and strategies that shape the future of excellence in organizations. In this introductory exploration, we embark on a journey into these advanced topics, delving into integration, risk-based approaches, supply chain management, sustainability, and the transformative impact of Quality 4.0 and Industry 4.0. These topics exemplify the dynamic nature of quality management, offering fresh perspectives and innovative solutions to navigate the evolving landscape of quality assurance and control.

A. Quality Management Systems Integration: Achieving Synergy in Excellence

Quality management systems (QMS) integration represents a sophisticated approach to enhancing organizational efficiency, effectiveness, and compliance by harmonizing various quality-related processes and standards within an organization. This integration ensures that quality is embedded throughout an organization's operations, fostering a culture of continuous improvement and excellence. In this in-depth exploration, we delve into the complex world of QMS integration, examining its significance, methodologies, challenges, and the transformative benefits it offers to organizations striving for excellence.

The Significance of QMS Integration:

1. **Efficiency:** Integration streamlines quality-related processes, reducing redundancy and inefficiencies. It enables organizations to allocate resources more effectively.

2. **Consistency:** A unified QMS ensures consistent application of quality standards and practices across all departments and functions.

3. **Compliance:** Integration helps organizations comply with multiple standards, regulations, and industry-specific requirements, reducing the risk of non-compliance.

4. **Continuous Improvement:** QMS integration supports a culture of continuous improvement by providing a holistic view of quality performance and enabling data-driven decision-making.

5. **Competitiveness:** Organizations with integrated QMS can respond more swiftly to market changes and customer

demands, enhancing their competitiveness.

Key Components of QMS Integration:

1. **Standardization:** Adopting standardized quality frameworks, such as ISO 9001, as a foundation for integration.

2. **Data Integration:** Consolidating quality-related data from various sources, systems, and departments into a central repository.

3. **Process Mapping:** Identifying and mapping key quality-related processes to understand their interdependencies.

4. **Cross-Functional Collaboration:** Encouraging collaboration among different departments and functions to align quality goals.

5. **Technology Integration:** Implementing integrated software solutions that facilitate data sharing and process automation.

6. **Performance Metrics:** Defining key performance indicators (KPIs) and metrics to measure the effectiveness of integrated processes.

Challenges in QMS Integration:

1. **Complexity:** Integrating diverse quality standards and processes can be complex, requiring meticulous planning and execution.

2. **Resistance to Change:** Employees and departments may resist changes to established processes and systems.

3. **Data Security:** Ensuring the security and confidentiality of integrated data is crucial, especially in regulated industries.

4. **Resource Constraints:** Integration efforts can be resource-intensive, requiring investments in technology and training.

5. **Sustainability:** Maintaining integrated systems and processes over the long term requires ongoing commitment and support.

Benefits of QMS Integration:

1. **Improved Efficiency:** Reduced duplication and streamlined processes lead to increased efficiency and cost savings.

2. **Enhanced Quality:** Integrated systems enable organizations to identify and address quality issues more effectively, resulting in higher product and service quality.

3. **Compliance:** Organizations can more easily meet regulatory requirements and industry standards.

4. **Innovation:** Integration fosters a culture of innovation by providing a foundation for data analysis and continuous improvement initiatives.

5. **Customer Satisfaction:** Consistent quality and improved responsiveness to customer needs lead to higher customer

satisfaction.

Conclusion:

QMS integration is a strategic imperative for organizations seeking to excel in today's competitive and highly regulated business environment. It empowers organizations to enhance efficiency, consistency, and compliance while fostering a culture of continuous improvement. By addressing the challenges and embracing the transformative benefits of QMS integration, organizations can position themselves for sustained success and excellence in quality management.

B. Risk-based Quality Management: Proactive Excellence in a Dynamic World

Risk-based quality management (RBQM) represents a modern and proactive approach to ensuring the quality and safety of products, services, and processes within organizations. It involves systematically identifying, assessing, and mitigating risks that could impact quality, compliance, or patient safety. RBQM is especially prevalent in industries such as healthcare, pharmaceuticals, and manufacturing, where regulatory scrutiny and patient or consumer safety are paramount. In this in-depth exploration, we delve into the world of risk-based quality management, examining its significance, methodologies, benefits, and the critical role it plays in navigating the complexities of a dynamic business landscape.

The Significance of Risk-based Quality Management:

1. **Proactive Risk Mitigation:** RBQM allows organizations to identify potential risks before they materialize, enabling proactive mitigation efforts.

2. **Enhanced Quality:** By focusing on high-risk areas, RBQM ensures that critical quality aspects receive the necessary attention and resources.

3. **Compliance:** RBQM helps organizations comply with regulations by systematically addressing risks associated with non-compliance.

4. **Resource Optimization:** It allows organizations to allocate resources more effectively by prioritizing risk-mitigation efforts.

5. **Patient and Consumer Safety:** In healthcare and pharmaceuticals, RBQM is crucial for ensuring patient safety by identifying and managing risks associated with medical products.

Key Components of Risk-based Quality Management:

1. **Risk Identification:** Identifying potential risks that could impact product quality, patient safety, or compliance.

2. **Risk Assessment:** Evaluating the severity and likelihood of identified risks to prioritize them effectively.

3. **Risk Mitigation:** Developing and implementing strategies to reduce or eliminate high-priority risks.

4. **Monitoring and Control:** Continuously monitoring risk factors and adapting risk mitigation strategies as needed.

5. **Documentation and Reporting:** Maintaining detailed records of risk assessment and mitigation efforts for regulatory compliance and transparency.

Challenges in Risk-based Quality Management:

1. **Data Availability:** Access to accurate and relevant data for risk assessment can be a challenge, especially in complex organizations.

2. **Complexity:** Managing a wide range of risks across multiple functions and departments can be complex and resource-intensive.

3. **Regulatory Expectations:** Meeting regulatory expectations for RBQM can be demanding, requiring clear documentation and evidence of risk management efforts.

4. **Cultural Shift:** Implementing RBQM may require a cultural shift within organizations, emphasizing the importance of risk

awareness and proactive mitigation.

Benefits of Risk-based Quality Management:

1. **Early Risk Identification:** RBQM enables early identification of potential risks, allowing organizations to take preventive measures.

2. **Resource Efficiency:** It optimizes resource allocation by focusing efforts on high-priority risks.

3. **Quality Enhancement:** By addressing high-risk areas, RBQM enhances overall product and service quality.

4. **Compliance:** RBQM helps organizations meet regulatory requirements and expectations for risk management.

5. **Patient and Consumer Safety:** In healthcare and pharmaceuticals, RBQM is essential for ensuring the safety of patients and consumers.

Conclusion:

Risk-based quality management represents a forward-looking and strategic approach to quality assurance and compliance. In an ever-changing and complex business environment, organizations must be proactive in identifying and addressing risks that could impact their products, services, and reputation. By embracing the principles and methodologies of RBQM, organizations can not only enhance their quality and safety measures but also ensure compliance with regulatory requirements, positioning themselves for sustained success and excellence in quality management.

C. Quality in Supply Chain Management: Building Resilience and Excellence

Quality in supply chain management is a critical component of modern business operations. It involves ensuring that products and materials consistently meet or exceed defined quality standards throughout their journey from suppliers to end customers. Effective quality management in the supply chain not only ensures product integrity but also supports efficiency, compliance, and customer satisfaction. In this in-depth exploration, we delve into the world of quality in supply chain management, examining its significance, challenges, methodologies, and the pivotal role it plays in building resilience and excellence in today's globalized business landscape.

The Significance of Quality in Supply Chain Management:

1. **Product Integrity:** Quality assurance in the supply chain ensures that products meet quality standards, reducing the risk of defects, recalls, and customer complaints.

2. **Efficiency:** Effective quality management streamlines supply chain processes, minimizing disruptions, delays, and excess

costs related to quality issues.

3. **Compliance:** Quality control supports adherence to regulatory requirements and industry standards, reducing the risk of legal and regulatory consequences.

4. **Customer Satisfaction:** High-quality products delivered on time contribute to customer satisfaction and loyalty.

5. **Risk Mitigation:** Proactive quality management helps identify and mitigate risks, such as supply chain disruptions or product recalls.

Key Components of Quality in Supply Chain Management:

1. **Supplier Qualification:** Assessing and selecting suppliers based on their quality capabilities, track record, and adherence to quality standards.

2. **Quality Control Procedures:** Implementing quality control measures and inspections at various stages of the supply chain to identify and address quality issues.

3. **Traceability:** Implementing systems and processes that allow for the tracking and tracing of products and materials throughout the supply chain.

4. **Data Analytics:** Utilizing data analytics to monitor and analyze quality-related data, identify trends, and make

informed decisions.

5. **Collaboration:** Collaboration with suppliers, logistics partners, and other stakeholders to align quality goals and processes.

Challenges in Quality in Supply Chain Management:

1. **Globalization:** Managing quality across a global supply chain with diverse suppliers and regulatory environments can be complex.

2. **Data Integration:** Integrating data from various systems and sources for effective quality monitoring and reporting.

3. **Supplier Reliability:** Ensuring that suppliers consistently meet quality standards and deliver on time.

4. **Risk Management:** Identifying and mitigating risks, such as supply chain disruptions, natural disasters, or geopolitical issues, that could impact quality.

5. **Regulatory Compliance:** Navigating a complex web of regulations and standards in different regions and industries.

Benefits of Quality in Supply Chain Management:

1. **Product Integrity:** Consistently high-quality products and materials reduce the risk of defects and recalls.

2. **Efficiency:** Streamlined supply chain processes lead to cost savings and reduced disruptions.

3. **Customer Satisfaction:** Delivering quality products on time enhances customer satisfaction and loyalty.

4. **Risk Mitigation:** Proactive quality management helps identify and address risks before they escalate.

5. **Compliance:** Meeting regulatory requirements and industry standards reduces the risk of legal and regulatory consequences.

Conclusion:

Quality in supply chain management is a strategic imperative in today's interconnected and fast-paced business environment. Organizations that prioritize and effectively manage quality throughout their supply chain are better positioned to build resilience, enhance customer satisfaction, reduce risks, and achieve operational excellence. By addressing the challenges and embracing the methodologies of quality in supply chain management, organizations can create a competitive advantage while safeguarding their reputation and bottom line.

D. Sustainable Quality Practices: Nurturing Excellence for Today and Tomorrow

Sustainable quality practices represent a holistic approach to quality management that goes beyond traditional metrics and considerations. They encompass not only the pursuit of product or service excellence but also the responsible stewardship of resources, environmental preservation, and long-term social and economic viability. Sustainable quality practices are increasingly recognized as essential in a world facing environmental challenges and heightened awareness of corporate social responsibility. In this in-depth exploration, we delve into the world of sustainable quality practices, examining their significance, principles, implementation strategies, and the transformative impact they have on organizations striving for excellence while safeguarding the planet and society.

The Significance of Sustainable Quality Practices:

1. **Environmental Responsibility:** Sustainable quality practices align with environmental stewardship, minimizing negative impacts on ecosystems, natural resources, and climate.

2. **Social Responsibility:** They address social and ethical considerations, including fair labor practices, diversity and inclusion, and community engagement.

3. **Economic Viability:** Sustainability practices promote long-term economic health by reducing waste, improving

efficiency, and enhancing brand reputation.

4. **Regulatory Compliance:** Organizations must increasingly comply with sustainability-related regulations and reporting requirements.

5. **Customer and Stakeholder Expectations:** Customers and stakeholders often expect organizations to demonstrate commitment to sustainability.

Key Principles of Sustainable Quality Practices:

1. **Integration:** Sustainability should be integrated into an organization's core values, strategy, and daily operations.

2. **Life Cycle Thinking:** Consider the environmental and social impacts of products and services throughout their entire life cycle, from design to disposal.

3. **Continuous Improvement:** Embrace a culture of continuous improvement to reduce environmental impacts and enhance social responsibility.

4. **Transparency and Reporting:** Communicate sustainability efforts transparently through reporting and disclosure mechanisms.

5. **Stakeholder Engagement:** Engage with stakeholders, including employees, customers, suppliers, and communities,

to understand and address their sustainability concerns.

Implementation Strategies for Sustainable Quality Practices:

1. **Environmental Management Systems (EMS):** Implementing EMS, such as ISO 14001, to manage and reduce environmental impacts systematically.

2. **Circular Economy:** Adopting principles of the circular economy, including recycling, reusing, and reducing waste.

3. **Sustainable Sourcing:** Sourcing materials and products from suppliers committed to sustainability and ethical practices.

4. **Energy Efficiency:** Improving energy efficiency through technology upgrades, process optimization, and renewable energy adoption.

5. **Eco-Design:** Integrating eco-design principles into product development to minimize environmental impacts.

6. **Employee Engagement:** Engaging employees in sustainability initiatives and providing training on sustainable practices.

Challenges in Sustainable Quality Practices:

1. **Complexity:** Implementing sustainable practices can be complex, requiring changes in processes, technologies, and

cultures.

2. **Cost Considerations:** There may be initial costs associated with sustainability initiatives, although they often yield long-term savings.

3. **Regulatory Compliance:** Navigating and complying with evolving sustainability regulations and standards can be challenging.

4. **Consumer Awareness:** Meeting the expectations of increasingly informed and environmentally conscious consumers.

Benefits of Sustainable Quality Practices:

1. **Environmental Preservation:** Reduced environmental impacts, resource conservation, and mitigation of climate change.

2. **Social Impact:** Enhanced social responsibility, including fair labor practices and community engagement.

3. **Cost Savings:** Increased efficiency, waste reduction, and long-term economic viability.

4. **Reputation and Brand Enhancement:** Improved brand reputation and customer loyalty through sustainability initiatives.

5. **Regulatory Compliance:** Adherence to sustainability regulations and standards.

Conclusion:

Sustainable quality practices are at the intersection of environmental responsibility, social accountability, and economic viability. Organizations that embrace these practices not only reduce their environmental footprint and enhance their social impact but also position themselves for long-term success and resilience in an increasingly sustainability-focused world. By addressing the challenges and implementing the principles of sustainable quality practices, organizations can nurture excellence that not only benefits the present but also ensures a better future for generations to come.

E. Quality 4.0 and Industry 4.0: Transforming Excellence Through Technology

Quality 4.0 and Industry 4.0 represent revolutionary paradigms that are reshaping the way organizations operate and deliver products and services. Rooted in advanced technologies and digitalization, these concepts are driving unprecedented improvements in quality, efficiency, and competitiveness across industries. In this in-depth exploration, we delve into the world of Quality 4.0 and Industry 4.0, examining their significance, principles, impact, and the transformative role they play in shaping the future of excellence.

Industry 4.0: The Foundation of Transformation:

Industry 4.0 is a term coined to describe the fourth industrial revolution characterized by the integration of cyber-physical systems, the Internet of Things (IoT), big data analytics, artificial intelligence (AI), and other advanced technologies into industrial processes. Its key principles and components include:

1. **Interconnectivity:** Machines, devices, and systems communicate and collaborate with each other, enabling real-time data sharing and decision-making.

2. **Information Transparency:** Access to data and information is democratized, providing visibility across the entire value chain.

3. **Technical Assistance:** AI and machine learning enhance decision-making, diagnostics, and problem-solving capabilities.

4. **Decentralized Decision-Making:** Cyber-physical systems operate autonomously, making localized decisions based on real-time data.

Quality 4.0: The Evolution of Quality Management:

Quality 4.0 builds on the foundations of Industry 4.0, applying its principles and technologies to the domain of quality management. It seeks to transform traditional quality practices by leveraging digital tools and data-driven insights. Key aspects of Quality 4.0 include:

1. **Data-Driven Decision-Making:** Quality decisions are based on real-time data and analytics, improving accuracy and responsiveness.

2. **Predictive Quality:** Machine learning and AI are used to predict and prevent quality issues before they occur.

3. **Digital Twins:** Digital replicas of products and processes enable virtual testing, optimization, and quality control.

4. **Automated Quality Monitoring:** Sensors and IoT devices continuously monitor quality parameters, providing immediate feedback.

5. **Enhanced Traceability:** Blockchain and secure databases ensure end-to-end traceability of products and their quality attributes.

The Impact of Quality 4.0 and Industry 4.0:

1. **Efficiency:** Automation and data-driven decision-making enhance operational efficiency, reducing waste and costs.

2. **Quality Improvement:** Real-time monitoring and predictive

analytics lead to improved product quality and fewer defects.

3. **Innovation:** Digital twins and collaborative design facilitate product and process innovation.

4. **Customer Satisfaction:** Enhanced quality and customization capabilities result in higher customer satisfaction.

5. **Competitive Advantage:** Organizations that embrace these paradigms gain a competitive edge in the global market.

Challenges in Implementing Quality 4.0 and Industry 4.0:

1. **Technology Adoption:** Integrating new technologies and systems can be complex and costly.

2. **Data Security:** Protecting sensitive data in a connected environment is paramount.

3. **Change Management:** Embracing a digital transformation often requires cultural and organizational changes.

4. **Skilled Workforce:** There is a growing need for a workforce with digital and technical skills.

Benefits of Quality 4.0 and Industry 4.0:

1. **Improved Quality:** Enhanced quality control and predictive capabilities result in higher product quality.

2. **Efficiency:** Automation and data-driven processes lead to cost

savings and improved resource allocation.

3. **Innovation:** The ability to rapidly prototype and test new products and processes drives innovation.

4. **Sustainability:** Greater efficiency and reduced waste contribute to sustainability efforts.

5. **Competitiveness:** Organizations that adopt these paradigms gain a competitive advantage.

Conclusion:

Quality 4.0 and Industry 4.0 are transforming the landscape of quality management and industrial processes. By embracing these paradigms, organizations can not only achieve higher quality and efficiency but also position themselves for long-term success and competitiveness in a rapidly evolving technological landscape. The integration of digitalization, data analytics, and advanced technologies promises to shape the future of excellence across industries.

CHAPTER 12

Case Studies and Success Stories

Case studies and success stories serve as invaluable sources of wisdom and inspiration, offering real-world insights into the triumphs, challenges, and strategies employed by organizations across diverse industries. These narratives provide a window into the practical application of knowledge, showcasing how businesses have navigated complex terrain, overcome obstacles, and achieved excellence. In this introductory exploration, we embark on a journey through case studies and success stories, unearthing the blueprints that illuminate the path to success, innovation, and resilience.

A. Real-world Implementations of Quality Management: Lessons from Excellence

Quality management isn't merely a theoretical concept; it thrives in the realm of practical application, where organizations across industries implement its principles and frameworks to achieve tangible results. These real-world implementations of quality management serve as beacons of excellence, demonstrating how commitment to quality can drive innovation, enhance efficiency, and elevate customer satisfaction. In this in-depth exploration, we delve into a myriad of real-world implementations, shedding light on their strategies, challenges, and the invaluable lessons they offer.

Diverse Industry Applications:

1. **Toyota's Lean Manufacturing:** Toyota revolutionized the automotive industry by implementing Lean principles, emphasizing waste reduction, continuous improvement, and employee involvement.

2. **GE's Six Sigma:** General Electric's widespread adoption of Six Sigma methodologies led to substantial quality improvements, cost savings, and enhanced customer satisfaction.

3. **Healthcare Quality Improvement:** Hospitals and healthcare systems worldwide have embraced quality management to reduce medical errors, improve patient outcomes, and optimize operational efficiency.

4. **Pharmaceutical Quality Control:** Pharmaceutical companies implement stringent quality control measures to ensure the safety and efficacy of their products, complying with rigorous regulatory standards.

5. **Aerospace Industry Standards:** The aerospace sector adheres to stringent quality standards to ensure the reliability

and safety of aircraft and space systems.

Common Strategies:

1. **Customer Focus:** Customer satisfaction remains a central goal, driving organizations to tailor their products and services to meet and exceed customer expectations.

2. **Data-Driven Decision-Making:** Utilizing data analytics to identify trends, track performance, and make informed quality-related decisions.

3. **Continuous Improvement:** Embracing a culture of continuous improvement by empowering employees to suggest and implement process enhancements.

4. **Quality Assurance:** Implementing robust quality assurance practices to prevent defects and ensure product consistency.

5. **Standardization:** Establishing standardized processes, procedures, and guidelines to maintain quality across the organization.

Challenges and Lessons Learned:

1. **Resistance to Change:** Overcoming resistance to change is a recurring challenge in quality management initiatives, emphasizing the importance of effective change management strategies.

2. **Resource Allocation:** Efficient resource allocation is crucial; organizations must balance investment in quality initiatives with the expected returns.

3. **Regulatory Compliance:** Meeting regulatory requirements demands meticulous documentation, adherence to standards, and rigorous quality control.

4. **Cultural Shift:** Ingraining a quality-focused culture requires strong leadership, employee engagement, and communication.

5. **Data Security:** Protecting sensitive data, especially in the age of digitalization, necessitates robust cybersecurity measures.

Outcomes and Benefits:

1. **Enhanced Quality:** Real-world implementations consistently result in improved product or service quality, driving customer satisfaction.

2. **Efficiency and Cost Savings:** Streamlined processes and reduced defects lead to cost savings and operational efficiency.

3. **Innovation:** Organizations often experience increased innovation and agility as a result of quality management practices.

4. **Compliance:** Stringent adherence to quality standards ensures

compliance with regulatory requirements.

5. **Sustainability:** Quality management practices often contribute to sustainability efforts by reducing waste and environmental impact.

Conclusion:

Real-world implementations of quality management are testaments to the transformative power of excellence. They exemplify the capacity of organizations to adapt, evolve, and excel by embracing quality principles and methodologies. The lessons learned from these practical applications continue to guide businesses worldwide on their journey to achieving enduring quality and success.

B. Industry-specific Case Studies: Tailored Excellence for Diverse Sectors

Industry-specific case studies offer a deep dive into how quality management principles are applied within specific sectors. These real-world examples showcase the nuances, challenges, and strategies unique to each industry, providing valuable insights into how organizations achieve excellence within their respective contexts. In this comprehensive exploration, we delve into industry-specific case studies, examining how quality management is customized and deployed across various sectors.

Automotive Industry: Lean Manufacturing at Toyota

One of the most renowned industry-specific case studies is Toyota's application of Lean Manufacturing principles in the automotive sector. Toyota revolutionized the industry by embracing concepts such as Just-In-Time production, continuous improvement (Kaizen), and respect for employees. This approach not only improved quality but also reduced waste, increased efficiency, and elevated customer satisfaction.

Key Takeaways:

- **Lean Principles:** The application of Lean principles, including waste reduction and process optimization, can drive quality improvements and cost savings in manufacturing.

- **Employee Involvement:** Engaging employees in continuous improvement initiatives fosters a culture of quality excellence.

- **Supply Chain Collaboration:** Collaborating closely with suppliers to ensure quality in the entire value chain is vital.

Pharmaceutical Industry: Quality Control and Compliance

In the pharmaceutical sector, quality management is synonymous with safety and regulatory compliance. Case studies in this industry often focus on how organizations ensure product safety, efficacy, and compliance with stringent regulations such as Good Manufacturing Practices (GMP).

Key Takeaways:

- **Regulatory Compliance:** Strict adherence to regulatory standards is non-negotiable for pharmaceutical companies to ensure product quality and patient safety.

- **Quality Control:** Robust quality control measures, including validation and testing, are essential to prevent defects and maintain consistency.

- **Documentation:** Meticulous documentation and record-keeping are imperative to demonstrate compliance.

Healthcare: Quality Improvement in Hospitals

In healthcare, quality management is a matter of life and death. Case studies in this sector typically revolve around initiatives to reduce medical errors, improve patient outcomes, and optimize operational efficiency in hospitals and healthcare systems.

Key Takeaways:

- **Patient Safety:** Ensuring patient safety is paramount, and quality management practices such as root cause analysis and process improvement are crucial.

- **Data-Driven Decisions:** Healthcare organizations increasingly rely on data analytics to identify trends, monitor performance, and make informed quality-related decisions.

- **Employee Engagement:** Engaging healthcare professionals in quality improvement initiatives is vital for success.

Aerospace Industry: Stringent Standards and Safety

The aerospace sector demands uncompromising quality and safety. Case studies in aerospace often highlight how organizations meet stringent quality standards to ensure the reliability and safety of aircraft and space systems.

Key Takeaways:

- **Regulatory Oversight:** The aerospace industry operates under extensive regulatory oversight, requiring meticulous compliance and documentation.

- **Risk Management:** Identifying and mitigating risks in complex systems is essential to maintaining quality and safety.

- **Supplier Quality:** Collaborating with high-quality suppliers is vital for aerospace organizations.

Food and Beverage: Ensuring Quality and Safety

Quality management in the food and beverage industry revolves around ensuring product safety, consistency, and compliance with food safety regulations. Case studies often explore how organizations maintain quality from farm to table.

Key Takeaways:

- **Food Safety:** Rigorous adherence to food safety standards is crucial to prevent contamination and ensure consumer safety.

- **Supply Chain Traceability:** Ensuring traceability throughout the supply chain is essential to respond to recalls and quality issues promptly.

- **Continuous Testing:** Regular product testing and quality control checks are essential in this sector.

Conclusion:

Industry-specific case studies provide invaluable insights into the tailored approaches and best practices for quality management within distinct sectors. While the specific challenges and strategies may vary, the overarching theme remains the same: a commitment to excellence, safety, and customer satisfaction. These case studies offer a wealth of knowledge that organizations can leverage to improve their own quality management practices and achieve industry-specific success.

C. Challenges Faced and Overcome in Quality Management

Quality management is not without its share of challenges. Organizations striving for excellence encounter various obstacles along the path to maintaining and improving quality. However, the history of quality management is rich with examples of how these challenges have been addressed and overcome. In this comprehensive exploration, we delve into the common challenges faced in quality management and the strategies employed to conquer them.

1. Resistance to Change:

Challenge: Employees and stakeholders may resist changes in processes and systems associated with quality management initiatives. Resistance can stem from fear of the unknown, concerns about job security, or a preference for familiar routines.

Overcoming Strategies:

- **Effective Communication:** Transparent communication about the need for change, its benefits, and the support provided can alleviate resistance.

- **Engagement:** Involving employees in the decision-making process and demonstrating how their input is valued can foster a sense of ownership and buy-in.

- **Training and Education:** Providing training to equip employees with the skills and knowledge necessary for the new processes can boost confidence and reduce resistance.

2. Resource Allocation:

Challenge: Implementing robust quality management practices often requires significant investments in technology, training, and personnel. Resource constraints can impede progress.

Overcoming Strategies:

- **Prioritization:** Prioritize initiatives based on their potential impact on quality and align them with organizational goals.

- **Cost-Benefit Analysis:** Evaluate the potential return on investment (ROI) for quality improvement initiatives to justify resource allocation.

- **Incremental Implementation:** Implement changes in stages, allocating resources incrementally as results are achieved.

3. Regulatory Compliance:

Challenge: Meeting stringent regulatory requirements, which can vary by industry and region, is a constant challenge. Non-compliance can result in legal consequences and reputational damage.

Overcoming Strategies:

- **Expertise:** Employ regulatory experts who can interpret and navigate complex regulations and standards.

- **Documentation:** Maintain meticulous records and documentation to demonstrate compliance.

- **Continuous Monitoring:** Implement systems for ongoing monitoring and compliance assessment.

4. Cultural Shift:

Challenge: Shifting an organization's culture to one that prioritizes quality can be a long and challenging process. Resistance to cultural change is common.

Overcoming Strategies:

- **Leadership Commitment:** Strong leadership commitment to quality and modeling desired behaviors is essential.

- **Employee Engagement:** Involve employees in quality initiatives and provide opportunities for them to contribute ideas and feedback.

- **Education and Training:** Provide training and education to help employees understand the importance of quality and how they contribute to it.

5. Data Security:

Challenge: In an increasingly digital world, safeguarding sensitive quality-related data from cyber threats and breaches is a paramount concern.

Overcoming Strategies:

- **Cybersecurity Measures:** Implement robust cybersecurity measures, including encryption, access controls, and regular security audits.

- **Data Backup and Recovery:** Establish data backup and recovery procedures to ensure data integrity and availability.

- **Employee Awareness:** Train employees on cybersecurity best practices to reduce the risk of data breaches caused by human error.

6. Balancing Quality and Cost:

Challenge: Striking a balance between maintaining high-quality standards and controlling costs can be challenging, especially in competitive markets.

Overcoming Strategies:

- **Continuous Improvement:** Embrace a culture of continuous improvement to identify cost-saving opportunities without compromising quality.

- **Supplier Collaboration:** Collaborate closely with suppliers to optimize costs while maintaining quality.

- **Technology Adoption:** Utilize technology, such as automation and data analytics, to improve efficiency and reduce costs.

Conclusion:

Challenges in quality management are inevitable, but they are not insurmountable. Organizations that succeed in overcoming these challenges do so by embracing change, allocating resources strategically, staying compliant, fostering a quality-centric culture, ensuring data security, and finding the delicate balance between quality and cost. These strategies, often guided by experience and best practices, demonstrate the resilience and adaptability of organizations committed to excellence in quality management.

D. Innovations and Lessons Learned in Quality Management

In the ever-evolving landscape of quality management, innovation and continuous improvement are essential drivers of excellence. Organizations that have embraced innovation have not only overcome challenges but have also set new standards for quality, efficiency, and customer satisfaction. In this comprehensive exploration, we delve into the innovations that have shaped the field of quality management and the valuable lessons learned along the way.

1. Total Quality Management (TQM):

Innovation: Total Quality Management (TQM) is a comprehensive approach that focuses on involving all employees in the continuous improvement of processes, products, and services. TQM emphasizes customer satisfaction, employee engagement, and data-driven decision-making.

Lessons Learned:

- **Cultural Transformation:** TQM taught us that a culture of quality is essential for success. It's not just a set of tools or techniques but a mindset that permeates the organization.

- **Customer-Centricity:** TQM's strong focus on customer needs and feedback highlighted the importance of aligning quality efforts with customer satisfaction.

- **Employee Involvement:** Engaging employees in quality initiatives empowers them to contribute to improvements and fosters a sense of ownership.

2. Lean Six Sigma:

Innovation: Lean Six Sigma combines the principles of Lean (waste reduction) and Six Sigma (defect reduction) to create a powerful approach for process improvement. It emphasizes data analysis, process optimization, and efficiency.

Lessons Learned:

- **Data-Driven Decision-Making:** Lean Six Sigma underscored the importance of basing decisions on data and metrics to identify root causes and solutions.

- **Efficiency and Waste Reduction:** The focus on eliminating waste and optimizing processes demonstrated that quality improvements can lead to significant cost savings.

- **Structured Problem Solving:** The DMAIC (Define, Measure, Analyze, Improve, Control) methodology provided a structured framework for tackling complex problems.

3. Industry 4.0 and Quality 4.0:

Innovation: The advent of Industry 4.0 and Quality 4.0 leverages digital technologies, data analytics, and automation to transform quality management. These innovations enable real-time monitoring, predictive analytics, and digital twins for quality control.

Lessons Learned:

- **Data's Value:** Industry 4.0 and Quality 4.0 emphasize the immense value of data. Lessons include the importance of data security, quality data collection, and data-driven decision-making.

- **Predictive Maintenance:** These innovations highlight the power of predictive maintenance in reducing downtime and improving product quality.

- **Agility:** Industry 4.0 and Quality 4.0 promote agility and adaptability, showing that organizations must be ready to embrace change and innovation continually.

4. Sustainable Quality Practices:

Innovation: Sustainable quality practices incorporate environmental and social responsibility into quality management. These practices promote sustainability, ethical sourcing, and corporate social responsibility.

Lessons Learned:

- **Triple Bottom Line:** Sustainable quality practices emphasize the triple bottom line, considering environmental, social, and economic impacts.

- **Consumer Consciousness:** Increasingly, consumers prioritize sustainable products and ethical practices, highlighting the importance of aligning quality with sustainability.

- **Regulatory Scrutiny:** Organizations must navigate evolving sustainability regulations and standards, necessitating adaptability and transparency.

5. Collaborative Quality Management:

Innovation: Collaborative quality management involves not only internal teams but also collaboration with suppliers and partners in the value chain. It fosters a culture of quality across organizations.

Lessons Learned:

- **Supply Chain Resilience:** Collaborative quality management underscores the importance of supply chain resilience and quality assurance throughout the value chain.

- **Transparency:** Open communication and transparency with suppliers and partners are crucial for maintaining consistent quality.

- **Shared Responsibility:** This innovation shows that quality is a shared responsibility, and organizations must work together to achieve excellence.

Conclusion:

Innovations in quality management have reshaped the field, bringing forth new methodologies, mindsets, and technologies. The lessons learned from these innovations emphasize the importance of data, customer-centricity, cultural transformation, and adaptability. They underscore the notion that quality management is a dynamic and evolving discipline that thrives on continuous improvement and innovation. By embracing these innovations and their associated lessons, organizations can navigate the ever-changing landscape of quality management and achieve enduring excellence.

CHAPTER 13

Quality Management in IT Projects

In today's technology-driven world, Information Technology (IT) projects have become the backbone of innovation and efficiency for organizations across the globe. Whether it's developing cutting-edge software solutions, implementing complex system upgrades, or building robust IT infrastructures, the success of these projects hinges on one crucial factor—quality.

Quality management in IT projects is not merely a best practice; it is the cornerstone of ensuring that IT initiatives meet their objectives, deliver value, and align with the overarching goals of the organization. This chapter delves into the intricacies of managing quality within the realm of IT projects, exploring the principles, methodologies, and best practices that IT professionals and project managers must embrace.

We will journey through the essence of quality in IT projects, uncovering how it influences software development, system implementations, and the deployment of IT infrastructure. We will delve into the realm of quality assurance and control, exploring methodologies to ensure that IT projects adhere to the highest standards. Real-world case studies will shed light on successful IT project quality management, demonstrating the tangible benefits that stem from a rigorous commitment to quality.

In an age where technology drives progress, the ability to master quality management in IT projects is an indispensable skill. Whether you're a seasoned IT professional or a project manager looking to enhance your IT project's success rate, this chapter serves as your guide to achieving excellence in the dynamic world of IT project management.

Let's embark on this journey into the realm of Quality Management in IT Projects, where every keystroke, every line of code, and every system component contributes to the foundation of a successful digital future.

A. Discuss the Application of Quality Management Principles in IT Project Management

Quality management principles are indispensable when it comes to Information Technology (IT) project management. IT projects, whether they involve software development, system implementation, or IT infrastructure upgrades, are complex endeavors with the potential for significant impact on an organization's operations. Ensuring that these projects meet or exceed expectations is paramount, and this can be achieved by integrating quality management principles into every phase of IT project management.

1. Clear Definition of Project Objectives:

At the outset of an IT project, defining clear and measurable objectives is fundamental to quality management. These objectives should align with the organization's strategic goals and stakeholder expectations. Quality objectives need to be specific, measurable, achievable, relevant, and time-bound (SMART). This clarity ensures that all project activities are focused on achieving the desired outcomes.

2. Stakeholder Engagement:

Quality management involves not only meeting technical specifications but also addressing the needs and expectations of stakeholders. Engaging stakeholders from the beginning helps in defining quality criteria, setting expectations, and incorporating their feedback throughout the project lifecycle. This ensures that the final deliverables align with stakeholders' requirements.

3. Robust Project Planning:

A well-structured project plan is essential for managing quality in IT projects. The plan should include detailed schedules, resource allocations, risk assessments, and a quality management plan. The quality management plan outlines the processes, standards, and metrics that will be used to ensure quality at every stage of the project.

4. Quality Assurance (QA):

Quality assurance in IT project management involves proactive steps to prevent defects or issues from occurring. It includes processes such as code reviews, design validations, and adherence to industry best practices. QA activities are conducted throughout the project's life cycle to catch and address issues early, reducing the cost and effort required for corrections later on.

5. Quality Control (QC):

Quality control focuses on identifying and rectifying defects or deviations from quality standards. This involves systematic testing, inspections, and verification activities. Automated testing tools and manual checks are used to ensure that the project's outputs meet predefined quality criteria.

6. Continuous Improvement:

The principles of continuous improvement from methodologies like Lean and Six Sigma play a crucial role in IT project quality management. This involves regularly assessing project processes, identifying areas for enhancement, and implementing improvements. Continuous improvement fosters a culture of excellence and ensures that the project team learns from its experiences.

7. Documentation and Traceability:

Comprehensive documentation is a key component of quality management in IT projects. It includes requirements documentation, test plans, issue logs, and change control records. Traceability ensures that every aspect of the project is well-documented, making it easier to track progress, assess compliance, and identify the root causes of any issues.

8. Metrics and Key Performance Indicators (KPIs):

Quality management relies on the collection and analysis of relevant metrics and KPIs. These measurements provide insights into project performance, quality levels, and adherence to standards. Common IT project KPIs include defect density, code coverage, on-time delivery, and customer satisfaction.

9. Risk Management:

Effective risk management is vital for quality assurance in IT projects. Identifying potential risks and developing risk mitigation strategies helps prevent quality issues and project delays. By proactively addressing risks, IT project managers can maintain quality standards even in the face of unexpected challenges.

In conclusion, the application of quality management principles in IT project management is essential for delivering successful projects that meet stakeholder expectations and align with organizational goals. By incorporating quality into every aspect of the project lifecycle, from planning to execution to monitoring and improvement, IT professionals can ensure that their projects achieve the highest levels of quality and reliability.

B. Ensuring the Quality of Software Development:

Quality in software development is about delivering software that meets or exceeds customer expectations, functions as intended, and is reliable and maintainable. To ensure software quality, consider the following:

1. **Clear Requirements:** Start with well-defined and documented requirements. Ensure that all stakeholders have a shared understanding of what the software should accomplish.

2. **Software Architecture:** Design a robust software architecture that supports scalability, maintainability, and performance. Properly structured code is easier to test and maintain.

3. **Coding Standards:** Enforce coding standards and best practices. Use code reviews to catch issues early, and employ static code analysis tools to identify potential problems.

4. **Testing:** Implement a comprehensive testing strategy that includes unit testing, integration testing, system testing, and user acceptance testing. Automated testing can help detect

defects early and ensure consistent testing procedures.

5. **Bug Tracking and Resolution:** Establish a bug tracking system to log and prioritize defects. Timely resolution of issues is crucial to maintaining software quality.

6. **Documentation:** Maintain thorough documentation, including user manuals and technical documentation. This aids in onboarding, troubleshooting, and future enhancements.

7. **Version Control:** Use version control systems to manage code changes and ensure that the correct versions of code are deployed.

8. **Security:** Prioritize security throughout the development process. Conduct security assessments and penetration testing to identify vulnerabilities.

9. **User Feedback:** Solicit feedback from end-users to identify usability and functionality issues. Continuously improve the software based on user input.

10. **Performance Optimization:** Monitor software performance and optimize code and infrastructure as needed. Address bottlenecks to ensure optimal user experience.

Ensuring the Quality of System Implementation:

System implementation involves deploying software and

hardware components into the production environment. Ensuring quality during this phase is crucial to prevent disruptions and maintain system reliability:

1. **Deployment Planning:** Develop a detailed deployment plan that outlines the steps, resources, and responsibilities for the implementation process.

2. **Testing Environments:** Create staging or test environments that mirror the production environment. Test the deployment thoroughly in these environments before moving to production.

3. **Backup and Rollback Plans:** Implement backup and recovery plans to minimize downtime and data loss. Have a well-defined rollback plan in case issues arise during deployment.

4. **Change Management:** Implement change management processes to control and document changes made during implementation. Ensure that changes are authorized and properly tested.

5. **Monitoring and Alerts:** Set up monitoring tools and alerts to detect and respond to performance issues or anomalies during and after deployment.

6. **Training:** Provide training to the operations team and end-

users to ensure that they are proficient in using the newly implemented system.

7. **Documentation:** Document the implementation process, configurations, and any changes made during deployment. This documentation is crucial for maintenance and troubleshooting.

8. **Post-Implementation Review:** Conduct a post-implementation review to evaluate the success of the deployment, identify lessons learned, and address any outstanding issues.

Ensuring the Quality of IT Infrastructure Projects:

IT infrastructure projects involve building, upgrading, or maintaining an organization's hardware and network infrastructure. Quality in IT infrastructure is vital for the stability and reliability of IT operations:

1. **Capacity Planning:** Perform thorough capacity planning to ensure that the infrastructure can handle current and future demands. Avoid over-provisioning or under-provisioning resources.

2. **Hardware Selection:** Choose reliable hardware components from reputable vendors. Ensure redundancy for critical components to minimize single points of failure.

3. **Network Design:** Design a robust network architecture that provides high availability, security, and efficient data flow. Consider factors like load balancing and failover.

4. **Security Measures:** Implement security best practices, including firewalls, intrusion detection systems, and encryption protocols, to protect the infrastructure from cyber threats.

5. **Backup and Disaster Recovery:** Establish backup and disaster recovery procedures to safeguard data and minimize downtime in the event of system failures or disasters.

6. **Performance Testing:** Conduct performance testing to ensure that the infrastructure can handle anticipated workloads and traffic levels.

7. **Scalability:** Design the infrastructure to be scalable, allowing for easy expansion as the organization grows.

8. **Documentation:** Maintain detailed documentation of the infrastructure configuration, network diagrams, and operational procedures. This documentation is essential for troubleshooting and future upgrades.

9. **Regular Maintenance:** Implement a schedule for regular maintenance, updates, and patch management to keep the infrastructure secure and up to date.

10. **Monitoring:** Set up monitoring tools to continuously monitor the health and performance of the infrastructure. Proactively address issues as they arise.

In summary, ensuring the quality of software development, system implementation, and IT infrastructure projects involves meticulous planning, testing, documentation, and ongoing maintenance. Quality should be embedded in every phase of these projects to deliver reliable and high-performing IT solutions that meet organizational needs.

C. Include case studies illustrating successful IT project quality management.

Case Study 1: Agile Development in Action

Background: A global e-commerce company embarked on a project to overhaul its customer-facing website, aiming to improve user experience and boost sales. The project involved a complex web application with multiple integrations, and it needed to be completed swiftly to stay competitive.

Quality Management Approach: The project team adopted Agile methodologies, with a focus on iterative development and continuous feedback. Regular sprint reviews allowed stakeholders to provide input, and automated testing was integrated into the development pipeline to catch defects early.

Success Factors:

- Collaboration: Cross-functional teams collaborated closely, fostering communication among developers, designers, and business stakeholders.

- Customer Feedback: Continuous feedback loops allowed the team to align the product with customer expectations.

- Test Automation: Automated testing reduced manual testing effort and improved software reliability.

- Iterative Improvement: Frequent retrospectives led to process improvements, making each sprint more efficient.

Outcome: The project was completed ahead of schedule, with a 20% increase in website traffic and a 15% boost in conversion rates. Quality management practices, including Agile methodologies and automated testing, played a crucial role in the project's success.

Case Study 2: Infrastructure Upgrade with Zero Downtime

Background: A large financial institution needed to upgrade its data center infrastructure to enhance security and performance. The challenge was to accomplish this without any service disruption to customers.

Quality Management Approach: The project team implemented meticulous planning and risk assessment. They set up a mirrored data center to ensure redundancy and failover capabilities. Load testing was conducted to validate the new infrastructure's performance under heavy loads.

Success Factors:

- Risk Mitigation: Comprehensive risk analysis and contingency planning minimized the chances of downtime.

- Redundancy: The mirrored data center allowed for seamless failover in case of unexpected issues.

- Load Testing: Rigorous load testing ensured that the infrastructure could handle peak workloads.

Outcome: The infrastructure upgrade was executed with zero unplanned downtime. Customers experienced uninterrupted service, and the enhanced security and performance improved overall customer satisfaction.

Case Study 3: GDPR Compliance and Data Protection

Background: A multinational technology company needed to comply with the General Data Protection Regulation (GDPR) to safeguard customer data and avoid hefty fines. This required extensive changes to data handling processes and systems.

Quality Management Approach: The project team conducted a thorough audit of data processing activities, identifying areas of non-compliance. They implemented data encryption, access controls, and privacy impact assessments. Continuous monitoring and audit trails were put in place to ensure ongoing compliance.

Success Factors:

- Compliance Expertise: The team included GDPR experts and legal counsel to interpret and implement the regulation effectively.

- Transparency: Communication with customers about data handling and privacy measures enhanced trust.

- Data Governance: Strict data governance policies ensured data accuracy, security, and compliance.

Outcome: The company achieved GDPR compliance, protecting customer data and avoiding regulatory fines. Customers appreciated the transparency and commitment to data privacy, enhancing the company's reputation.

These case studies showcase different aspects of IT project quality management, including Agile development practices, infrastructure resilience, and regulatory compliance. They highlight the importance of tailored quality management approaches for specific project requirements and objectives.

CHAPTER 14

IT Service Quality Management

IT Service Quality Management is a critical discipline within the Information Technology (IT) industry that focuses on delivering high-quality services to users and customers. In today's digital age, where organizations heavily rely on technology to drive their operations, ensuring the reliability, efficiency, and effectiveness of IT services is paramount. IT Service Quality Management encompasses a set of practices, processes, and frameworks designed to monitor, measure, and continually improve the quality of IT services, thereby aligning technology solutions with business needs and customer expectations.

This chapter explores the dimensions of IT service quality, strategies for measuring and enhancing service quality, and best practices for managing IT services effectively. It delves into the significance of IT service quality in meeting the demands of modern businesses and ensuring a seamless experience for end-users. Through a comprehensive examination of ITIL (Information Technology Infrastructure Library) and related frameworks, this chapter aims to equip IT professionals with the knowledge and tools necessary to excel in the realm of IT service quality management.

A. Exploring IT Service Quality Dimensions and Their Significance

In the realm of Information Technology (IT), service quality is a multifaceted concept that extends beyond mere technical functionality. IT service quality is defined by various dimensions, each of which plays a crucial role in determining the overall satisfaction of users and customers. Exploring these dimensions and understanding their significance is fundamental to delivering IT services that meet or exceed user expectations.

Here, we delve into the key dimensions of IT service quality and their significance:

1. Reliability:

- *Significance:* Reliability is the cornerstone of IT service quality. It measures the consistency and dependability of IT services. Users expect systems and applications to be available and operational when needed.

- *Impact:* High reliability ensures minimal downtime and disruptions, contributing to user productivity and business continuity. It fosters trust among users and reduces the risk of service failures.

2. Responsiveness:

- *Significance:* Responsiveness gauges the timeliness of IT support and issue resolution. Users value quick responses to their queries or problems.

- *Impact:* Prompt responses enhance user satisfaction, minimize downtime, and facilitate rapid problem resolution. They also demonstrate a commitment to user needs.

3. Security:

- *Significance:* Security is paramount in the digital age, especially for sensitive data and critical systems. IT services must protect against threats and vulnerabilities.

- *Impact:* Robust security measures instill confidence in users and safeguard data integrity. Failure in this dimension can lead to data breaches, financial losses, and reputational damage.

4. Performance:

- *Significance:* Performance measures the speed and efficiency of IT services. Users expect fast response times and smooth operation.

- *Impact:* High performance enhances user experience, productivity, and efficiency. Poor performance can lead to frustration and decreased productivity.

5. Availability:

- *Significance:* Availability assesses how often IT services are accessible. Users rely on services being available 24/7.

- *Impact:* Continuous availability is crucial for businesses with global operations and round-the-clock demands. Downtime can result in lost revenue and customer dissatisfaction.

6. Serviceability:

- *Significance:* Serviceability relates to ease of maintenance, upgrades, and scalability of IT services. Complex or cumbersome systems can be costly to manage.

- *Impact:* Serviceable systems are cost-effective to maintain and can adapt to changing business needs. They reduce the total cost of ownership.

7. User Experience:

- *Significance:* User experience encompasses the ease of use, intuitiveness, and overall satisfaction of interacting with IT services.

- *Impact:* A positive user experience fosters user adoption, reduces training costs, and increases user satisfaction.

8. Compliance:

- *Significance:* Compliance refers to adherence to industry standards, regulations, and best practices. Different industries have specific compliance requirements.

- *Impact:* Non-compliance can lead to legal issues, fines, and reputational damage. Meeting compliance standards is essential for certain sectors like healthcare and finance.

Understanding these dimensions and their significance allows IT professionals to prioritize efforts and resources effectively. Balancing these dimensions ensures that IT services not only meet technical specifications but also align with user expectations and business goals, ultimately contributing to the success of an organization.

B. Explaining How IT Professionals Can Measure and Improve Service Quality

Measuring and improving service quality in Information Technology (IT) is essential to ensure that IT services align with user expectations and business objectives. IT professionals employ various methods and strategies to gauge service quality and continuously enhance it. Here, we delve into how IT professionals can measure and improve service quality effectively:

1. Define Key Performance Indicators (KPIs):

- *Measurement:* Begin by identifying and defining relevant Key Performance Indicators (KPIs) that align with service quality dimensions, such as reliability, responsiveness, and security.

KPIs should be quantifiable and measurable.

- *Improvement:* Regularly monitor KPIs to track performance and identify areas that require improvement. For instance, if responsiveness is a critical dimension, track response times to user requests.

2. Conduct User Surveys:

- *Measurement:* Gather user feedback through surveys and questionnaires. Ask users to rate their satisfaction with various aspects of IT services, including reliability, performance, and user experience.

- *Improvement:* Analyze survey results to pinpoint areas of dissatisfaction or concern. Use this feedback to prioritize improvements and address specific pain points.

3. Implement ITIL and Service Management Frameworks:

- *Measurement:* Adopt frameworks like ITIL (Information Technology Infrastructure Library) that provide guidance on IT service management best practices. These frameworks often include predefined metrics for service quality.

- *Improvement:* Implementing ITIL or similar frameworks helps standardize IT service processes and metrics. It enables IT professionals to focus on areas identified for improvement and optimize service delivery.

4. Service Level Agreements (SLAs):

- *Measurement:* Establish clear Service Level Agreements (SLAs) that outline performance expectations and commitments to users. SLAs should include defined metrics and targets.

- *Improvement:* Regularly review SLAs to ensure they align with evolving business needs and user expectations. If service levels are consistently falling short, reevaluate processes and resource allocation.

5. Incident and Problem Management:

- *Measurement:* Monitor incidents and problems related to IT services. Track the frequency, severity, and resolution times of incidents and problems.

- *Improvement:* Implement robust incident and problem management processes to swiftly address issues. Analyze incident and problem data to identify recurring issues and implement preventive measures.

6. Continuous Monitoring and Analysis:

- *Measurement:* Employ monitoring tools and systems to continuously track the performance and availability of IT services. Collect real-time data on service health.

- *Improvement:* Use monitoring data to proactively detect and address potential issues before they impact users. Implement predictive analytics to foresee service disruptions.

7. Root Cause Analysis (RCA):

- *Measurement:* When incidents occur, conduct thorough Root Cause Analysis (RCA) to determine the underlying causes. Identify whether issues are systemic or isolated.

- *Improvement:* Address root causes to prevent the recurrence of similar incidents. Implement preventive measures and process improvements based on RCA findings.

8. Benchmarking:

- *Measurement:* Compare your organization's IT service quality against industry benchmarks and peer organizations. Benchmarking helps identify performance gaps.

- *Improvement:* Emulate best practices from organizations with superior service quality. Use benchmarking data to set realistic improvement goals.

9. Training and Skill Development:

- *Measurement:* Assess the competence of IT staff in service delivery and management. Regularly evaluate their knowledge and skills.

- *Improvement:* Invest in training and skill development programs to enhance the capabilities of IT professionals. Well-trained staff can better contribute to service quality.

10. Automation and Innovation: - *Measurement:* Leverage automation and innovation to streamline IT processes and reduce the likelihood of errors. - *Improvement:* Automate routine tasks and explore innovative solutions to optimize service delivery. Automation can lead to increased efficiency and reduced downtime.

By employing these measurement and improvement strategies, IT professionals can continuously enhance service quality, align IT services with business needs, and meet or exceed user expectations. This iterative approach ensures that IT services remain responsive, reliable, secure, and efficient, ultimately contributing to the success of the organization.

C. Highlighting Best Practices for Managing IT Service Quality with ITIL and Related Frameworks

Managing IT service quality is a critical aspect of ensuring that Information Technology (IT) aligns with business objectives and meets user expectations. One of the most widely adopted frameworks for IT service management is ITIL (Information Technology Infrastructure Library). In addition to ITIL, several related frameworks and best practices can significantly contribute to managing IT service quality effectively. Let's explore these best practices:

1. ITIL (Information Technology Infrastructure Library):

- **Service Strategy:** ITIL emphasizes aligning IT services with business needs. Start by defining clear service strategies that reflect the organization's objectives.

- **Service Design:** Design services with a focus on quality, reliability, and scalability. Consider factors like Service Level Agreements (SLAs) and Continual Service Improvement (CSI).

- **Service Transition:** Ensure a smooth transition of new or modified services into production. Rigorous testing and validation are essential to maintain quality.

- **Service Operation:** Monitor and manage IT services to ensure they meet predefined quality standards. Incident and problem management play crucial roles in maintaining service quality.

- **Continual Service Improvement (CSI):** Regularly assess service performance, gather feedback, and initiate improvements. CSI is central to maintaining and enhancing service quality over time.

2. COBIT (Control Objectives for Information and Related Technologies):

- COBIT provides a comprehensive framework for governance and management of enterprise IT. It emphasizes aligning IT with business goals, which is fundamental to ensuring service quality.

- Implement COBIT's governance and management practices to establish control objectives and metrics that contribute to service quality.

- Use COBIT's maturity models to assess and improve IT processes, thereby enhancing service quality and reliability.

3. ISO/IEC 20000:

- ISO/IEC 20000 is an international standard specifically for IT service management. It defines a set of requirements for establishing, implementing, maintaining, and continually improving a service management system.

- Adhering to ISO/IEC 20000 ensures that IT service quality is in line with globally recognized standards. Organizations can achieve certification to demonstrate their commitment to service quality.

4. Six Sigma:

- Six Sigma principles and methodologies can be applied to improve IT service quality by minimizing defects and variations in processes.

- Use Six Sigma's DMAIC (Define, Measure, Analyze, Improve, Control) approach to identify, measure, and rectify issues affecting service quality.

5. Agile and DevOps:

- Agile and DevOps practices emphasize collaboration, automation, and continuous improvement in software development and IT operations.

- Adopt Agile and DevOps principles to accelerate software development, enhance collaboration, and ensure the rapid delivery of high-quality IT services.

6. Lean IT:

- Lean IT principles focus on eliminating waste, improving efficiency, and delivering value to customers.

- Implement Lean IT practices to optimize IT processes, reduce costs, and enhance service quality.

7. Risk Management:

- Effective risk management is crucial for maintaining service quality. Identify potential risks, assess their impact, and develop mitigation strategies.

- Integrate risk management into IT service management practices to ensure proactive handling of potential disruptions.

8. Knowledge Management:

- Implement knowledge management practices to capture and share best practices, lessons learned, and solutions. A well-managed knowledge base can expedite issue resolution and improve service quality.

9. Performance Metrics:

- Define and track performance metrics aligned with service quality goals. Metrics may include availability, response time, and customer satisfaction scores.

- Regularly analyze performance data to identify trends and areas for improvement.

10. Automation and Self-Service: - Automate routine IT tasks and provide self-service options to users. This reduces manual errors and enhances service efficiency, contributing to improved service quality.

By embracing these best practices and frameworks, IT professionals can establish a robust foundation for managing IT service quality effectively. ITIL, COBIT, ISO/IEC 20000, Six Sigma, Agile, DevOps, Lean IT, risk management, knowledge management, performance metrics, and automation collectively enable organizations to maintain high-quality IT services that meet user needs and support overall business success.

CHAPTER 15

IT Regulatory Compliance and Quality

In today's digital age, the Information Technology (IT) landscape is governed by a complex web of regulations and standards aimed at safeguarding data, ensuring privacy, and maintaining the integrity of IT systems. Achieving and sustaining IT regulatory compliance is not only a legal requirement but also a fundamental aspect of quality assurance in IT operations. This chapter delves into the critical intersection of IT regulatory compliance and quality, shedding light on how IT organizations can meet compliance requirements while upholding the highest standards of service quality.

Key Points to Explore in this Chapter:

- **Understanding IT-Specific Regulations:** Gain insights into the diverse set of IT-specific regulations and standards that impact the industry. Explore key regulations such as GDPR (General Data Protection Regulation), HIPAA (Health Insurance Portability and Accountability Act), ISO/IEC 27001, and others, each with its own unique requirements.

- **Balancing Compliance and Quality:** Discover strategies for maintaining the delicate balance between adhering to regulatory frameworks and ensuring IT service quality. Explore how compliance efforts can actually enhance quality management practices.

- **Case Studies in Compliance:** Examine real-world case studies that illustrate successful compliance initiatives in the IT sector. Learn from organizations that have effectively navigated regulatory challenges while maintaining high-quality IT services.

As we dive into the intricacies of IT regulatory compliance and its profound impact on quality assurance, we will uncover the strategies, best practices, and practical insights that IT professionals need to uphold both legal requirements and the delivery of top-notch IT services.

A. Navigating IT Regulatory Landscape: GDPR, HIPAA, ISO/IEC 27001, and More

In the realm of Information Technology (IT), adherence to specific regulations and standards is not only a legal necessity but a paramount concern for safeguarding data, ensuring privacy, and maintaining the integrity of IT systems. This section explores several IT-specific regulations, standards, and compliance requirements, shedding light on their significance and impact on the IT industry.

1. GDPR (General Data Protection Regulation):

- **Significance:** GDPR, enacted by the European Union (EU), is a globally influential regulation that governs the protection of personal data. It empowers individuals with greater control over their data and places strict requirements on organizations handling personal data.

- **Compliance Requirements:** GDPR mandates transparency, consent, data minimization, and the appointment of Data Protection Officers (DPOs). It also stipulates severe penalties for data breaches and non-compliance.

2. HIPAA (Health Insurance Portability and Accountability Act):

- **Significance:** HIPAA is a U.S. regulation specifically targeting the healthcare industry. It ensures the confidentiality and security of patient health information (PHI) while promoting electronic health records (EHR) adoption.

- **Compliance Requirements:** HIPAA requires healthcare organizations to implement security measures, conduct risk assessments, and provide training to protect PHI. It also includes provisions for breach reporting.

3. ISO/IEC 27001:

- **Significance:** ISO/IEC 27001 is an international standard for

Information Security Management Systems (ISMS). It provides a comprehensive framework for managing information security risks and ensuring the confidentiality, integrity, and availability of information assets.

- **Compliance Requirements:** Compliance with ISO/IEC 27001 involves risk assessments, security policy development, access control, and continuous monitoring. It emphasizes a systematic approach to information security.

4. NIST Cybersecurity Framework:

- **Significance:** Developed by the U.S. National Institute of Standards and Technology (NIST), this framework helps organizations manage and reduce cybersecurity risk. It offers guidelines and best practices applicable to various industries.

- **Compliance Requirements:** NIST Cybersecurity Framework consists of five functions: Identify, Protect, Detect, Respond, and Recover. Organizations must assess their cybersecurity posture, implement controls, and establish incident response procedures.

5. PCI DSS (Payment Card Industry Data Security Standard):

- **Significance:** PCI DSS applies to organizations handling payment card data. It aims to protect cardholder data from breaches and fraud. Compliance is crucial for e-commerce and financial services.

- **Compliance Requirements:** PCI DSS sets out requirements for securing cardholder data, including network security, encryption, access controls, and regular security assessments.

6. ITIL (Information Technology Infrastructure Library):

- **Significance:** While not a regulation, ITIL is a framework that offers best practices for IT service management. It helps IT organizations deliver high-quality services and align with business objectives.

- **Compliance Requirements:** ITIL emphasizes processes like Incident Management, Problem Management, and Change Management. Organizations can voluntarily adopt ITIL principles to improve service quality.

Navigating this intricate web of regulations and standards requires a deep understanding of their implications and meticulous planning. IT professionals must stay abreast of evolving compliance requirements to ensure that their organizations not only meet legal obligations but also maintain the highest standards of IT service quality.

B. Balancing Act: Maintaining IT Quality within Regulatory Frameworks

Maintaining quality in IT while adhering to regulatory frameworks is a complex but necessary endeavor. IT organizations must navigate a web of regulations, each with its own set of requirements, while ensuring that the services and products they deliver meet high-quality standards. Here's how IT organizations can achieve this delicate balance:

1. Thorough Understanding of Regulations:

- IT organizations must invest time and resources in understanding the specific regulations that apply to their industry and geography. This includes GDPR, HIPAA, ISO/IEC 27001, and others.

- Establish a dedicated compliance team or designate compliance officers responsible for interpreting and implementing regulations within the organization.

2. Risk Assessment:

- Conduct comprehensive risk assessments to identify vulnerabilities and potential compliance gaps. This involves evaluating current IT systems, data handling practices, and security measures.

- Prioritize risks and focus efforts on addressing high-impact areas that are critical for both compliance and quality.

3. Robust Policies and Procedures:

- Develop and implement policies and procedures that align with regulatory requirements. These policies should cover data handling, access control, incident response, and more.

- Ensure that these policies are well-documented, accessible to all employees, and regularly reviewed and updated.

4. Training and Awareness:

- Provide ongoing training and awareness programs for employees regarding compliance and quality standards. All staff should understand their roles and responsibilities in maintaining compliance and quality.

- Conduct regular drills and simulations to test incident response and ensure that employees can respond effectively to potential compliance breaches.

5. Data Protection Measures:

- Implement robust data protection measures, including encryption, access controls, and data anonymization techniques. These measures not only help with compliance but also safeguard data quality.

- Regularly monitor and audit data handling practices to ensure that sensitive information remains secure and accurate.

6. Continuous Monitoring and Auditing:

- Establish continuous monitoring processes to track compliance and quality metrics. Use automated tools to detect anomalies and potential breaches in real-time.

- Conduct internal and external audits regularly to assess compliance and quality performance. Address any issues promptly and proactively.

7. Incident Response Plans:

- Develop and test incident response plans that outline steps to take in the event of a compliance or quality breach. These plans should include communication strategies, containment measures, and post-incident analysis.

- Learn from past incidents to improve processes and prevent future breaches.

8. Documentation and Records Management:

- Maintain detailed records of compliance efforts, audit results, and quality assessments. Proper documentation is crucial for demonstrating adherence to regulations and quality standards.

- Implement records management practices that align with regulatory requirements, such as data retention and disposal policies.

9. External Expertise:

- Consider seeking external expertise in compliance and quality management. Consultants and auditing firms with expertise in specific regulations can provide valuable insights and guidance.

10. Continuous Improvement: - Embrace a culture of continuous improvement. Regularly review and update compliance and quality processes based on evolving regulations, industry best practices, and lessons learned from incidents.

Balancing IT quality and regulatory compliance is an ongoing process that requires vigilance and adaptability. By integrating compliance requirements into their quality management systems and proactively addressing both, IT organizations can build trust with customers, protect sensitive data, and ensure the longevity of their operations.

C. Case Studies in Successful Compliance and Quality Practices in IT

In the realm of Information Technology (IT), where compliance and quality are paramount, success stories often revolve around organizations that have effectively navigated complex regulatory landscapes while maintaining high standards of service and product quality. Here are a few illustrative case studies of such successes:

Case Study 1: GDPR Compliance at XYZ Corporation

Background: XYZ Corporation, a multinational tech company, was faced with the challenge of complying with the General Data Protection Regulation (GDPR), a strict data protection regulation enforced by the European Union. Failure to comply would not only result in substantial fines but also damage the company's reputation.

Approach:

- XYZ Corporation formed a dedicated GDPR compliance team comprising legal experts, IT professionals, and data protection officers.

- They conducted a comprehensive audit of their data handling practices, identified areas of non-compliance, and initiated corrective actions.

- The company invested in data encryption, access controls, and data anonymization tools to secure personal data.

Results:

- XYZ Corporation achieved full GDPR compliance ahead of the deadline.

- The company's proactive approach to data protection not only ensured legal compliance but also enhanced customer trust.

- This success became a cornerstone of their marketing efforts, showcasing their commitment to data privacy.

Case Study 2: ISO/IEC 27001 Certification at ABC Solutions

Background: ABC Solutions, an IT services provider, sought to distinguish itself in a competitive market by demonstrating a commitment to information security and quality. They pursued ISO/IEC 27001 certification, an international standard for information security management systems.

Approach:

- ABC Solutions engaged a certified ISO/IEC 27001 auditor to assess their existing information security measures.

- They established an information security management system (ISMS) that included policies, procedures, and controls.

- The company conducted extensive employee training on information security and quality management.

Results:

- ABC Solutions received ISO/IEC 27001 certification, signaling their dedication to information security.

- Clients were reassured by the certification, leading to an increase in business opportunities.

- The company experienced fewer security incidents, resulting in cost savings and enhanced customer satisfaction.

Case Study 3: ITIL Implementation at Tech Innovators Inc.

Background: Tech Innovators Inc., a software development company, aimed to improve the quality of its IT services. They adopted ITIL (Information Technology Infrastructure Library), a set of practices for IT service management, to standardize processes and enhance service quality.

Approach:

- Tech Innovators Inc. invested in ITIL training for their IT staff to ensure a common understanding of IT service management best practices.

- They redefined their service catalog, introduced incident management procedures, and established a robust change management process.

- Continuous monitoring and regular assessments ensured adherence to ITIL principles.

Results:

- Service quality improved significantly, with reduced downtime and faster incident resolution.

- The company experienced enhanced customer satisfaction as clients noted the improved reliability of their software.

- Tech Innovators Inc. achieved cost savings by optimizing resource allocation and reducing service disruptions.

These case studies highlight the importance of a proactive and holistic approach to compliance and quality management in IT. Organizations that prioritize compliance with regulations, standards, and quality practices not only avoid legal penalties but also gain a competitive edge, build trust with customers, and achieve operational excellence.

CHAPTER 16

IT Quality Metrics and Key Performance Indicators (KPIs)

In the dynamic and ever-evolving landscape of Information Technology (IT), the effective measurement and management of quality are vital for ensuring the delivery of reliable, secure, and high-performing IT services and products. To achieve this, IT professionals rely on a set of well-defined metrics and Key Performance Indicators (KPIs) that offer insights into the health, efficiency, and effectiveness of IT operations. This chapter delves into the world of IT Quality Metrics and KPIs, shedding light on their significance and how they empower IT organizations to monitor, evaluate, and continuously enhance their quality standards.

Effective IT Quality Metrics and KPIs go beyond mere data collection; they provide actionable information that guides decision-making, drives process improvements, and aligns IT strategies with organizational goals. From measuring the uptime of critical systems to assessing the success of cybersecurity initiatives, these metrics play a pivotal role in maintaining the integrity and excellence of IT services.

Throughout this chapter, we will explore a wide range of IT

Quality Metrics and KPIs, dissecting their practical applications, and showcasing how IT professionals can leverage them to optimize their operations, foster innovation, and, most importantly, ensure the satisfaction of end-users and stakeholders. Whether it's monitoring service desk response times, tracking software development cycle times, or evaluating network performance, the world of IT Quality Metrics and KPIs offers a comprehensive toolkit to enhance the quality and reliability of IT services in the digital age.

A. Exploring Specific Quality Metrics and KPIs Relevant to IT

In the realm of Information Technology (IT), quality metrics and Key Performance Indicators (KPIs) serve as compasses, guiding IT professionals towards achieving excellence in various aspects of their operations. These metrics are tailored to measure specific facets of IT services, systems, and processes, providing valuable insights into their performance and effectiveness. Below, we delve into a range of specific quality metrics and KPIs relevant to IT, shedding light on their significance and applications:

1. **Uptime and Availability Metrics:** These metrics assess the continuous availability of IT systems and services. They include measures like "percentage of uptime," "mean time between failures (MTBF)," and "mean time to recover

(MTTR)." High uptime percentages indicate system reliability and minimal service interruptions.

2. **Response and Resolution Times:** For IT service desks, response and resolution times are crucial. Metrics such as "average response time" and "average resolution time" help gauge the efficiency of IT support. Faster response and resolution times lead to improved user satisfaction.

3. **Incident and Problem Management Metrics:** These metrics track the handling of incidents and problems, including the number of incidents resolved, the recurrence of problems, and the time taken to resolve critical issues. They contribute to the overall quality of IT service delivery.

4. **Change Management Metrics:** Change management is pivotal in IT. Metrics related to change success rates, failed changes, and the time taken to implement changes help evaluate the impact of changes on system stability.

5. **Service Level Agreement (SLA) Compliance:** Measuring SLA compliance ensures that IT services meet the agreed-upon standards. Metrics include "SLA adherence rate" and "percentage of SLAs met," reflecting IT's commitment to service quality.

6. **Network Performance Metrics:** Network quality is paramount for seamless IT operations. Metrics such as

"network latency," "packet loss rate," and "bandwidth utilization" assess the efficiency and reliability of network infrastructure.

7. **Security Metrics:** IT security metrics focus on assessing the effectiveness of cybersecurity measures. These include "number of security breaches," "time to detect and respond to security incidents," and "vulnerability assessment results."

8. **Software Development Metrics:** For software development projects, metrics like "code quality" (evaluated through static code analysis), "defect density," and "lead time" help ensure the delivery of high-quality software products.

9. **Infrastructure Capacity and Performance Metrics:** These metrics measure the capacity and performance of IT infrastructure components like servers, storage, and databases. Metrics include "CPU utilization," "memory usage," and "storage capacity planning."

10. **User Satisfaction Metrics:** Ultimately, user satisfaction is a crucial measure of IT quality. Surveys, feedback, and Net Promoter Scores (NPS) help gauge how well IT services align with user expectations and needs.

By carefully monitoring and analyzing these IT quality metrics and KPIs, IT professionals can proactively identify areas for improvement, optimize resource allocation, and align IT strategies with organizational goals. These metrics not only enhance the quality of IT services but also contribute to the overall success of an organization in today's technology-driven world.

B. Using IT Metrics to Measure and Improve Quality

Measuring and improving quality is a fundamental aspect of IT management, and IT professionals rely on a range of metrics and Key Performance Indicators (KPIs) to achieve these goals. Here, we explore how IT professionals can effectively use these metrics to assess and enhance quality in various IT domains:

1. **Identify Baseline Performance:** The first step is to establish baseline measurements using relevant metrics. IT professionals need to know where they stand in terms of quality before they can make improvements. For example, by tracking metrics like uptime and response times, they can understand the current state of IT service reliability and efficiency.

2. **Set Clear Quality Goals:** Once baselines are established, IT professionals should set clear quality goals. These goals should be specific, measurable, achievable, relevant, and time-bound (SMART). For instance, if the baseline for network latency is 20 milliseconds, a SMART goal might be to reduce it to 10 milliseconds within six months.

3. **Continuous Monitoring:** Metrics are most effective when they are continuously monitored. IT professionals should implement monitoring tools and practices to track the selected metrics in real-time or at regular intervals. This ensures that any deviations from quality standards are promptly identified.

4. **Root Cause Analysis:** When deviations occur, IT professionals should conduct root cause analysis to understand the underlying issues. Metrics alone may not provide the full picture, so qualitative analysis and investigation may be required. For instance, if there is a sudden increase in incident response times, the root cause analysis may reveal that the IT service desk is understaffed.

5. **Benchmarking:** Comparing metrics against industry benchmarks and best practices can provide valuable insights. IT professionals can assess whether their organization's performance is on par with or lags behind industry standards. Benchmarking can lead to targeted improvement efforts.

6. **Regular Reporting and Communication:** Metrics data should be regularly reported to relevant stakeholders, including IT management and business leaders. Transparent communication about the current state of quality, progress toward goals, and any challenges faced is essential for organizational alignment and support.

7. **Actionable Insights:** Metrics should not be viewed in

isolation; they should provide actionable insights. IT professionals should use metrics to identify specific areas for improvement and develop action plans. For example, if security incident metrics reveal a high number of phishing attacks, an action plan might include employee training on cybersecurity best practices.

8. **Iterative Improvement:** Quality improvement is an iterative process. After taking action based on metrics, IT professionals should reassess and measure the impact of their efforts. If the desired quality improvements are not achieved, adjustments to strategies and tactics may be necessary.

9. **Employee and Team Involvement:** Quality improvement is a collaborative effort. IT professionals should engage team members and employees in the process. Teams should understand the relevance of metrics to their work and take ownership of quality improvement initiatives.

10. **Technology and Tools:** Leveraging advanced monitoring and analytics tools can simplify the process of collecting, analyzing, and reporting on metrics. These tools can provide real-time insights and automate the measurement process, allowing IT professionals to focus on interpretation and action.

11. **Feedback Loops:** Encourage feedback loops within IT teams and with end-users. Feedback can provide qualitative insights that complement quantitative metrics. It helps in fine-tuning

IT processes and services to meet user expectations.

In summary, IT professionals use metrics and KPIs as valuable tools to measure and improve quality in various IT domains. By establishing baselines, setting goals, continuous monitoring, and taking actionable steps based on insights, IT teams can enhance the quality of IT services, systems, and processes, ultimately contributing to the success of their organizations. Quality management in IT is an ongoing journey, and metrics are the compass that guides continuous improvement efforts.

C. Practical Examples and Best Practices for Tracking IT Quality

Tracking IT quality is crucial for ensuring the reliability, performance, and security of IT services and systems. To effectively measure and monitor IT quality, IT professionals can implement practical examples and best practices:

1. **Service Availability Metrics:**

   - **Example:** Calculate the uptime percentage of critical services over a month. For instance, a critical web application should ideally be available 99.9% of the time (resulting in less than 43 minutes of downtime per month).

   - **Best Practice:** Set thresholds for acceptable uptime

levels and implement monitoring tools that provide real-time availability data. Automated alerts should notify IT teams when service availability falls below the defined threshold.

2. **Response Time Monitoring:**

- **Example:** Measure the response time of key IT services, such as login authentication or database queries, and record the average response time over a specified period.

- **Best Practice:** Use performance monitoring tools to capture response time data. Set performance baselines and proactively address deviations. Consider implementing synthetic transactions to simulate user interactions and monitor response times.

3. **Incident Resolution Metrics:**

- **Example:** Track the time it takes to resolve IT incidents, from initial report to resolution, and calculate the average resolution time for different incident categories.

- **Best Practice:** Implement an IT Service Management (ITSM) system to manage incidents and automate incident tracking. Define service level agreements

(SLAs) for incident resolution and regularly review performance against SLAs.

4. Change Success Rate:

- **Example:** Measure the success rate of changes and updates to IT systems and applications. Calculate the percentage of changes that were implemented without causing service disruptions.

- **Best Practice:** Implement a change management process that includes thorough testing, risk assessment, and rollback plans. Monitor and report on change success rates, and use lessons learned to improve change management practices.

5. Security Incident Metrics:

- **Example:** Track the number and severity of security incidents, such as malware infections or data breaches, over time. Categorize incidents based on their impact.

- **Best Practice:** Implement security information and event management (SIEM) systems to collect and analyze security event data. Regularly review incident trends and patterns to strengthen security measures and incident response capabilities.

6. **User Satisfaction Surveys:**

   - **Example:** Conduct regular surveys to gather feedback from end-users about their IT experiences, including application usability, system performance, and IT support.

   - **Best Practice:** Use standardized surveys with rating scales and open-ended questions. Analyze survey results to identify areas of improvement and prioritize action based on user feedback.

7. **Compliance Audits:**

   - **Example:** Conduct periodic compliance audits to assess adherence to regulatory and security standards, such as GDPR, HIPAA, or ISO/IEC 27001.

   - **Best Practice:** Develop audit checklists and schedules based on applicable standards. Assign responsibilities for audit preparation and remediation of non-compliance findings.

8. **Capacity Planning:**

   - **Example:** Monitor resource utilization (CPU, memory, storage) and project future capacity needs based on historical data.

- **Best Practice:** Implement capacity planning tools and predictive analytics to forecast resource requirements. Adjust capacity as needed to accommodate growth and ensure optimal performance.

9. **Patch and Vulnerability Management:**

   - **Example:** Keep track of software patches and vulnerabilities. Monitor the time taken to apply critical security patches after their release.

   - **Best Practice:** Implement vulnerability scanning tools to identify vulnerabilities in IT systems. Prioritize and expedite the application of critical patches to mitigate security risks.

10. **Continuous Improvement Logs:**

    - **Example:** Maintain a log of identified issues, improvement initiatives, and their outcomes. Document the impact of improvements on IT quality.

    - **Best Practice:** Create a centralized repository for continuous improvement records. Regularly review and assess the effectiveness of improvement efforts.

11. **Training and Skill Development:**

    - **Example:** Track the completion of training programs

and certifications for IT staff. Monitor skill development and competence levels.

- **Best Practice:** Use learning management systems to manage training programs and skill assessments. Ensure that IT professionals are up-to-date with relevant certifications and skills.

12. **Financial Metrics:**

- **Example:** Monitor IT spending against budgets and track the cost-effectiveness of IT initiatives.

- **Best Practice:** Implement financial management tools and practices to control IT costs. Regularly review and optimize IT budgets and expenses.

13. **User Support Metrics:**

- **Example:** Measure the time it takes to resolve user support requests, such as helpdesk tickets. Track user satisfaction with IT support services.

- **Best Practice:** Implement an ITIL-based service desk framework to standardize support processes. Use ticketing systems to monitor response times and user feedback.

Incorporating these practical examples and best practices into

IT quality tracking efforts enables IT professionals to maintain high standards of quality, proactively address issues, and continuously improve IT services and operations. These metrics provide valuable insights for decision-making and help align IT with organizational goals and user expectations.

CHAPTER 17

IT Quality Assurance vs. Quality Control

In the realm of Information Technology (IT), ensuring the delivery of high-quality products and services is paramount. IT Quality Assurance (QA) and Quality Control (QC) are two distinct but interconnected approaches that organizations employ to achieve this objective. While both share the common goal of delivering quality IT solutions, they operate at different stages of the software development and service delivery lifecycle.

Quality Assurance (QA) focuses on the processes and methodologies used during the development, implementation, and maintenance of IT systems. It emphasizes preventive measures and aims to establish robust processes that minimize the likelihood of defects and errors. QA is proactive and forward-looking, striving to identify and mitigate potential issues before they impact the end-users or the organization.

Quality Control (QC), on the other hand, is primarily concerned with the identification and rectification of defects and issues in IT products and services. It involves systematic testing, inspection, and monitoring activities to detect deviations from established quality standards. QC is reactive and concentrates on finding and fixing problems that have already occurred.

In this comprehensive exploration of IT Quality Assurance vs. Quality Control, we will delve deeper into these two vital facets of IT quality management. We will dissect their key differences, explore their respective roles and methodologies, and highlight how they complement each other in the pursuit of IT excellence. Additionally, we will provide practical insights and best practices for effectively implementing QA and QC in IT organizations, ensuring that the final IT deliverables meet the highest standards of quality, reliability, and user satisfaction.

A. Delving Deeper into the Distinction Between Quality Assurance and Quality Control in IT

In the dynamic landscape of Information Technology (IT), the distinction between Quality Assurance (QA) and Quality Control (QC) is vital, as each plays a unique and crucial role in ensuring the delivery of high-quality IT solutions. Let's explore the differences between these two approaches in greater detail:

1. Focus and Objectives:

- **Quality Assurance (QA):** QA is process-oriented. Its primary objective is to establish and maintain robust processes throughout the IT project lifecycle. QA aims to prevent defects and issues from occurring by emphasizing process improvements, adherence to best practices, and the implementation of standards. It is proactive in nature and seeks to identify and mitigate potential risks before they impact the project.

- **Quality Control (QC):** QC, on the other hand, is product-oriented. Its primary objective is to detect and rectify defects or issues in the final product or service. QC involves systematic testing, inspection, and monitoring activities to ensure that the end deliverables meet the established quality criteria. It is reactive and concentrates on identifying and addressing problems after they have occurred.

2. Timing and Stage:

- **Quality Assurance (QA):** QA activities are integrated into the entire IT project lifecycle, from planning and design to development and maintenance. QA processes are ongoing and continuous, ensuring that quality is ingrained in every phase of the project.

- **Quality Control (QC):** QC activities typically occur after the development phase of the project. Testing and inspection activities are performed on the final product or service to identify defects or deviations from quality standards.

3. Methodologies:

- **Quality Assurance (QA):** QA methodologies include process management, risk assessment, and process improvement techniques such as Six Sigma and Lean. QA also involves creating and maintaining documentation of best practices and standards.

- **Quality Control (QC):** QC methodologies encompass testing techniques, inspections, reviews, and audits. QC activities involve the identification of defects, issue tracking, and reporting.

4. Role and Responsibility:

- **Quality Assurance (QA):** QA is a responsibility shared by the entire project team and often involves dedicated QA professionals who ensure that processes are followed and standards are adhered to.

- **Quality Control (QC):** QC is typically carried out by dedicated testing and quality control teams who focus on identifying and addressing defects and issues in the product.

5. Outcome:

- **Quality Assurance (QA):** The outcome of effective QA is a well-defined and controlled process that minimizes the likelihood of defects and issues, resulting in a more predictable and efficient IT project.

- **Quality Control (QC):** The outcome of effective QC is a product or service that has undergone rigorous testing and inspection, ensuring that it meets the specified quality standards and is free from defects.

In conclusion, while QA and QC are distinct in their objectives and methodologies, they are complementary and essential components of a comprehensive IT quality management strategy. By integrating both QA and QC into IT projects, organizations can enhance the overall quality of their IT solutions, reduce risks, and ultimately deliver products and services that meet or exceed user expectations.

B. Roles, Processes, and Methodologies in Quality Assurance (QA) and Quality Control (QC) in IT

To gain a comprehensive understanding of Quality Assurance (QA) and Quality Control (QC) in Information Technology (IT), it's essential to explore the roles, processes, and methodologies associated with each approach.

Roles:

1. **Quality Assurance (QA):**

   - **QA Manager:** Oversees the QA process, defines QA strategies, and ensures that QA procedures are implemented.

   - **QA Team:** Comprised of QA analysts and testers who work collaboratively with project teams to enforce quality standards and best practices.

   - **Process Owners:** Responsible for specific processes within the project, ensuring compliance with defined standards and continuous process improvement.

2. **Quality Control (QC):**

   - **QC Tester:** Conducts testing and inspection activities to identify defects and deviations from quality standards in the product or service.

   - **QC Inspector:** Conducts detailed inspections of deliverables to ensure they meet established criteria.

   - **QC Auditor:** Performs audits to evaluate adherence to quality processes and standards.

Processes:

1. **Quality Assurance (QA):**

   - **Process Definition:** Define and document project processes and standards, including coding standards, development methodologies, and testing protocols.

   - **Process Implementation:** Enforce defined processes and standards throughout the project lifecycle.

   - **Process Monitoring:** Continuously monitor processes to identify areas for improvement and ensure compliance.

   - **Process Improvement:** Implement process enhancements and corrective actions based on monitoring results.

2. **Quality Control (QC):**

   - **Testing:** Execute various types of testing, including functional, regression, performance, and security testing, to identify defects in the product.

   - **Inspection:** Inspect project deliverables and code to verify they align with quality standards.

   - **Defect Tracking:** Identify, log, and prioritize defects, and track their resolution.

- **Validation:** Ensure that the final product meets predefined acceptance criteria.

Methodologies:

1. **Quality Assurance (QA):**

   - **Six Sigma:** A data-driven methodology focused on reducing defects and improving process efficiency.

   - **Lean:** A methodology that aims to minimize waste and maximize value within processes.

   - **ISO Standards:** Adherence to ISO standards such as ISO 9001 for quality management systems.

   - **Best Practices:** Implementing industry-recognized best practices in development and project management.

2. **Quality Control (QC):**

   - **Testing Methodologies:** Utilize various testing methodologies like manual, automated, and exploratory testing.

   - **Testing Tools:** Employ testing tools and frameworks for test automation and defect tracking.

   - **Inspection Checklists:** Develop checklists to

systematically inspect code, design, and project deliverables.

- **Compliance Audits:** Conduct audits to ensure adherence to regulatory and industry-specific standards.

Integration: QA and QC are complementary processes that work together to enhance IT project quality. QA ensures that robust processes are in place to prevent defects, while QC focuses on detecting and addressing defects in the product or service. Integration between the two involves feedback loops where QC findings inform QA process improvements, creating a continuous cycle of quality enhancement.

In summary, QA and QC are essential components of IT quality management, each with its defined roles, processes, and methodologies. When effectively integrated into IT projects, they ensure the delivery of high-quality IT solutions that meet user expectations and industry standards.

C. Balancing Quality Assurance (QA) and Quality Control (QC) for Optimal IT Quality Outcomes

Balancing Quality Assurance (QA) and Quality Control (QC) is crucial for achieving optimal quality outcomes in IT projects.

Both QA and QC play distinct roles in ensuring quality, and finding the right equilibrium between them is essential for project success.

1. Clear Role Definitions:

- **QA Focus:** QA primarily focuses on process-oriented activities. IT organizations should clearly define the responsibilities of the QA team in setting up processes, standards, and guidelines.

- **QC Focus:** QC, on the other hand, concentrates on product-oriented activities. Define the QC team's responsibilities related to testing, inspecting, and identifying defects.

2. Early Prevention vs. Post-Detection:

- **QA's Preventive Approach:** QA's primary objective is to prevent defects from occurring in the first place. This involves setting up robust processes, conducting reviews, and ensuring adherence to best practices.

- **QC's Detective Approach:** QC aims to detect defects after they have occurred. QC activities include testing, inspections, and audits to identify and rectify issues.

3. Collaboration and Communication:

- **Continuous Collaboration:** Encourage open communication and collaboration between QA and QC teams. Regular meetings and knowledge sharing help both teams understand project goals and align their efforts.

- **Feedback Loops:** Implement feedback loops where QC findings inform QA process improvements. For example, recurring defects detected by QC can trigger process enhancements by QA.

4. Flexibility and Adaptability:

- **Adaptation to Project Needs:** The balance between QA and QC may vary depending on the project's nature and stage. Agile projects, for instance, may require more frequent QC activities during development iterations.

- **Scalability:** Ensure that the QA and QC approach is scalable to meet project requirements. Larger projects may need more extensive QA processes and resources.

5. Risk Assessment:

- **Risk-Based Approach:** Conduct risk assessments to determine where to allocate QA and QC resources. High-risk areas may require more QC activities, while well-established processes may need less intense QA oversight.

- **Impact Analysis:** Assess the potential impact of defects on project objectives. This analysis can guide decisions on whether to focus efforts on prevention (QA) or detection and correction (QC).

6. Metrics and Key Performance Indicators (KPIs):

- **Measurement and Analysis:** Implement metrics and KPIs to evaluate the effectiveness of both QA and QC efforts. Monitor defect rates, process adherence, and customer satisfaction.

- **Continuous Improvement:** Use metrics to identify areas where the balance between QA and QC may need adjustment. If defects continue to arise, it may signal the need for more preventive measures (QA).

7. Resource Allocation:

- **Resource Allocation Strategy:** Allocate resources based on project size, complexity, and criticality. High-stakes projects may justify increased investment in both QA and QC.

- **Optimizing Costs:** Evaluate the cost-effectiveness of QA and QC activities. Avoid over-investing in either at the expense of project efficiency.

8. Regulatory and Compliance Requirements:

- **Compliance-Driven Balance:** In industries with stringent regulatory requirements (e.g., healthcare, finance), compliance-related QC activities may be more prominent.

However, QA remains essential for ensuring processes meet compliance standards.

9. Continuous Learning and Training:

- **Skill Enhancement:** Invest in training and skill development for both QA and QC teams. Continuous learning ensures that teams are equipped to handle evolving project challenges.

10. Feedback-Driven Improvement: - Iterative Process: Strive for an iterative improvement process where the balance between QA and QC evolves as the project progresses. Regular retrospectives can identify areas for adjustment.

Finding the optimal balance between QA and QC in IT projects is a dynamic process that requires ongoing evaluation and adaptation. By understanding their unique roles and collaborating effectively, IT organizations can enhance the overall quality of their deliverables while optimizing resource allocation and project efficiency.

CHAPTER 18

IT Quality Tools and Techniques

In the ever-evolving landscape of Information Technology (IT), the pursuit of quality is paramount. IT Quality Tools and Techniques play a pivotal role in ensuring that software, systems, and services meet the highest standards of performance, reliability, and security. This chapter delves into the arsenal of tools and techniques specifically tailored to the IT domain, equipping IT professionals with the means to enhance the quality of their deliverables and operations.

From identifying root causes of issues to optimizing processes and evaluating the effectiveness of IT services, this chapter unravels a comprehensive toolkit. These tools and techniques empower IT practitioners to proactively manage quality, mitigate risks, and drive continuous improvement. Whether you're a software developer, IT manager, or quality assurance specialist, this chapter will serve as a valuable resource for elevating the quality of IT projects and services.

A. Expanding the Toolkit: Quality Tools and Techniques for IT

In the fast-paced world of Information Technology (IT), where innovation and precision are the norm, the use of quality tools and techniques tailored to the IT domain is essential. These specialized tools help IT professionals ensure the reliability, efficiency, and security of software, systems, and services. In this section, we will explore the expansion of the toolkit, focusing on quality tools and techniques specifically applicable to IT.

1. **Pareto Analysis in IT:** Pareto Analysis, known as the 80/20 rule, is a valuable tool for identifying and prioritizing issues in IT projects and operations. IT teams can use this technique to allocate resources effectively, focusing on the most critical issues that impact quality.

2. **Fishbone Diagrams (Ishikawa Diagrams) in IT:** Fishbone diagrams are used to visualize the potential causes of a problem or issue. In IT, this technique helps in root cause analysis, allowing IT professionals to pinpoint the underlying factors contributing to quality issues, such as system crashes or software bugs.

3. **Root Cause Analysis (RCA) in IT:** RCA is a systematic process used to investigate and identify the root causes of problems in IT. It enables IT teams to develop effective corrective actions to prevent the recurrence of quality-related

issues.

4. **Statistical Process Control (SPC) in IT:** SPC involves monitoring and controlling IT processes using statistical methods. IT professionals can use control charts to ensure that IT processes, such as software development or system maintenance, remain within acceptable quality limits.

5. **IT-specific Software Testing Tools:** The IT industry offers a plethora of specialized software testing tools for quality assurance. These tools include automated testing frameworks, load testing software, and code analysis tools, all designed to enhance software quality.

6. **Quality Assurance Frameworks for IT:** Quality assurance frameworks like ITIL (Information Technology Infrastructure Library) provide comprehensive guidelines and best practices for managing IT services. ITIL, for instance, emphasizes service quality, incident management, and continuous improvement.

7. **Root Cause Analysis (RCA) Tools for IT:** RCA tools specific to IT help IT professionals investigate and resolve complex issues in IT infrastructure, software, and systems. These tools streamline the RCA process, facilitating quicker problem resolution.

8. **Configuration Management Tools:** Configuration

management tools are crucial for maintaining the quality and consistency of IT environments. They help IT teams track changes, manage assets, and ensure that configurations adhere to desired standards.

9. **Continuous Integration/Continuous Deployment (CI/CD) Tools:** CI/CD tools automate the integration and deployment of software changes, enhancing the quality of software development and minimizing errors.

10. **IT Monitoring and Alerting Systems:** Monitoring tools continuously track the performance of IT systems and services, providing real-time data and alerts to maintain optimal quality and availability.

11. **Quality Metrics and Key Performance Indicators (KPIs) for IT:** IT professionals use a range of quality metrics and KPIs to measure and improve quality. These may include metrics related to system uptime, response times, error rates, and customer satisfaction.

By incorporating these specialized tools and techniques into their IT practices, professionals can ensure that their IT projects, systems, and services meet and exceed quality expectations. This chapter will provide practical examples and guidance on how to effectively utilize these tools to drive quality improvement in the IT domain.

B. Applying Quality Tools to IT: Pareto Analysis, Fishbone Diagrams, and Root Cause Analysis

In the realm of Information Technology (IT), where complexity and precision are paramount, quality management is crucial. To tackle quality-related challenges, IT professionals often employ established quality tools and techniques adapted to the IT domain. This section delves into the IT-specific applications of three prominent tools: Pareto Analysis, Fishbone Diagrams (Ishikawa Diagrams), and Root Cause Analysis (RCA).

1. Pareto Analysis in IT:

- **Identifying Priority Issues:** Pareto Analysis, based on the 80/20 rule, is particularly useful in IT for identifying and prioritizing issues. IT professionals can gather data on problems, errors, or incidents and analyze them to determine which issues have the most significant impact on IT quality.

- **Resource Allocation:** Pareto Analysis allows IT teams to allocate resources effectively. By focusing on the vital few issues that contribute the most to quality problems, IT professionals can concentrate their efforts where they will have the greatest impact.

- **Example:** In IT, Pareto Analysis might reveal that 20% of software bugs are responsible for 80% of system crashes. By addressing this critical 20%, IT teams can significantly improve system stability.

2. Fishbone Diagrams (Ishikawa Diagrams) in IT:

- **Visualizing Root Causes:** Fishbone Diagrams are instrumental in visualizing the potential causes of a problem or issue. In IT, this tool helps IT professionals conduct comprehensive root cause analysis.

- **Problem Solving:** IT teams can use Fishbone Diagrams to explore various categories of potential causes, such as hardware, software, processes, or personnel. This structured approach facilitates problem-solving and identification of underlying issues.

- **Example:** When a software application experiences performance issues, a Fishbone Diagram can break down potential causes into categories like code quality, server capacity, database performance, and network latency.

3. Root Cause Analysis (RCA) in IT:

- **Investigating Complex Issues:** RCA is a systematic process used to investigate and identify the root causes of problems in IT. It is especially valuable for complex, recurring issues that impact IT quality.

- **Preventing Recurrence:** Once the root causes are identified, IT professionals can develop corrective actions to prevent the recurrence of quality-related problems. This proactive approach is essential for maintaining IT quality.

- **Example:** In IT, RCA can be applied to diagnose a network outage. It might reveal that the outage was caused by a misconfigured router, and the corrective action would involve reconfiguring the router and implementing change management processes to prevent similar issues.

IT-Specific Applications:

- **Software Development:** In software development, Pareto Analysis can identify the most critical defects to address. Fishbone Diagrams help developers understand the underlying causes of software issues, while RCA ensures that root causes are addressed to improve software quality.

- **IT Service Management:** ITIL frameworks often use these tools to analyze incidents and problems in service delivery. Pareto Analysis helps prioritize incident resolution, Fishbone Diagrams uncover service delivery bottlenecks, and RCA drives process improvements.

- **Network Management:** For network professionals, these tools assist in diagnosing network performance problems, pinpointing the root causes of network outages, and streamlining network configurations.

By applying these quality tools with a focus on IT-specific challenges, IT professionals can enhance the quality of software, systems, and services, resulting in more reliable and efficient IT operations.

C. Examples of Quality Improvement in IT Using Tools

Quality improvement in Information Technology (IT) is essential for ensuring the reliability, efficiency, and effectiveness of IT systems and services. IT professionals can employ various quality tools and techniques to enhance IT processes and deliver better results. Here, we provide examples of how IT professionals can use tools like Pareto Analysis, Fishbone Diagrams (Ishikawa Diagrams), and Root Cause Analysis (RCA) for quality improvement:

1. Pareto Analysis in IT:

Example: An IT support team notices a significant increase in the number of helpdesk tickets related to software issues. To prioritize their efforts, they gather data on the types of software problems reported. After performing Pareto Analysis, they discover that 20% of the reported issues, such as application crashes and data loss, are responsible for 80% of user dissatisfaction. By focusing on these critical issues, the IT team can allocate resources efficiently to resolve them promptly.

2. Fishbone Diagrams (Ishikawa Diagrams) in IT:

Example: A software development team is facing a recurring problem of delayed project deliveries. To identify the root causes, they create a Fishbone Diagram. Categories include development processes, communication, resource allocation, and external dependencies. After analysis, they discover that inadequate communication and unclear project requirements are significant contributors to delays. With this insight, they implement improved communication practices and requirements gathering processes, leading to on-time project deliveries.

3. Root Cause Analysis (RCA) in IT:

Example: A company experiences frequent network outages that disrupt business operations. An IT team conducts RCA to identify the root causes. After a thorough investigation, they discover that the primary cause is outdated network hardware. The corrective action involves upgrading the network equipment and implementing a proactive hardware maintenance schedule. As a result, network reliability improves, and downtime is significantly reduced.

These examples illustrate how IT professionals can leverage quality tools to:

- Prioritize efforts by identifying critical issues.

- Visualize potential causes and conduct structured analysis.

- Investigate complex problems to identify root causes.

- Implement corrective actions to prevent recurrence.

By incorporating these tools into their IT processes, professionals can enhance the quality of software development, IT services, and network management, leading to more robust and reliable IT systems that better meet business needs.

Conclusion

As we draw the final curtain on this journey through these pages, we invite you to reflect on the knowledge, insights, and discoveries that have unfolded before you. Our exploration of various subjects has been a captivating voyage into the depths of understanding.

In these chapters, we have ventured through the intricacies of numerous topics and examined the key concepts and findings that define these fields. It is our hope that you have found inspiration, enlightenment, and valuable takeaways that resonate with you on your own quest for knowledge.

Remember that the pursuit of understanding is an ever-evolving journey, and this book is but a milestone along the way. The world of knowledge is vast and boundless, offering endless opportunities for exploration and growth.

As you conclude this book, we encourage you to carry forward the torch of curiosity and continue your exploration of these subjects. Seek out new perspectives, engage in meaningful discussions, and embrace the thrill of lifelong learning.

We express our sincere gratitude for joining us on this intellectual adventure. Your curiosity and dedication to expanding your horizons are the driving forces behind our shared quest for wisdom and insight.

Thank you for entrusting us with a portion of your intellectual journey. May your pursuit of knowledge lead you to new heights and inspire others to embark on their own quests for understanding.

With sincere appreciation,

Nikhilesh Mishra, Author

Recap of Key Takeaways

As we journey through the diverse realms of quality management, it's essential to pause and reflect on the key takeaways that underpin the principles, frameworks, and practices discussed in this comprehensive guide. These takeaways serve as guiding lights, illuminating the path toward achieving and sustaining excellence in quality management. Let's recap these fundamental insights:

1. Quality Is Multifaceted and Ever-Evolving:

Quality is not a one-dimensional concept but a multifaceted one that encompasses product quality, process quality, service quality, and more. It evolves with changing customer expectations, technological advancements, and global dynamics.

2. Historical Evolution Shapes the Present:

Understanding the historical evolution of quality management, from its roots in craftsmanship to modern quality standards, provides valuable insights into its development and significance.

3. Key Concepts Are Building Blocks:

Quality standards and Total Quality Management (TQM) are foundational concepts that lay the groundwork for effective quality management. ISO standards and TQM principles emphasize the importance of systematic approaches and continuous improvement.

4. Principles Are the Heart of Quality Management:

Quality management principles, such as customer focus, leadership, engagement, process approach, and improvement, serve as guiding values that organizations must embody to achieve excellence.

5. Benefits Are Compelling, but Challenges Exist:

Quality management offers numerous benefits, including improved customer satisfaction, efficiency, and competitiveness. However, organizations must navigate challenges like resistance to change, resource allocation, and regulatory compliance.

6. Frameworks Offer Guidance:

Quality management frameworks, including ISO standards, Lean Six Sigma, and the Baldrige Excellence Framework, provide structured approaches to implementing quality management practices.

7. Planning and Strategy Are Essential:

Quality planning involves setting clear quality objectives, policies, and using tools like QFD and FMEA to ensure products and processes align with customer expectations. Strategic quality management aligns quality with organizational goals and culture.

8. Assurance and Control Differ in Focus:

Quality assurance focuses on preventing defects and ensuring compliance, while quality control centers on detecting and correcting defects through inspections and tests.

9. Tools Enhance Decision-Making:

Quality tools and techniques, such as Pareto Analysis, Fishbone Diagrams, and Statistical Process Control, provide data-driven insights for effective decision-making and problem-solving.

10. Total Quality Management (TQM) Is Holistic:

TQM is a comprehensive approach that emphasizes customer focus, employee involvement, continuous improvement, and cultural transformation to achieve excellence.

11. Quality Matters in Every Industry:

Quality management principles are applicable across industries, from manufacturing and healthcare to service sectors like finance and hospitality.

12. Regulatory Compliance Is a Must:

Quality management is intrinsically tied to regulatory compliance, with organizations needing to adhere to standards like ISO, FDA, and GMP to ensure product safety and consistency.

13. Advanced Topics Shape the Future:

Topics like quality systems integration, risk-based quality

management, sustainable practices, and Industry 4.0 (Quality 4.0) represent the future of quality management, driving innovation and competitiveness.

14. Case Studies Offer Real-world Wisdom:

Real-world case studies and success stories provide tangible examples of how organizations have implemented quality management principles to achieve excellence, highlighting strategies and lessons learned.

15. Innovation and Continuous Improvement Are Imperative:

Innovation, driven by data and technology, fuels continuous improvement in quality management. Embracing change and learning from successes and challenges are key to sustained excellence.

As we conclude this journey, remember that quality management is not a destination but an ongoing commitment to excellence. Embrace these key takeaways, adapt them to your organization's unique context, and let them guide your pursuit of enduring quality and customer satisfaction.

Nikhilesh Misha

The Future of Quality Management

The future of quality management is a dynamic and exciting landscape characterized by rapid technological advancements, evolving customer expectations, and the integration of quality into every facet of an organization's operations. As we peer into this future, we see several key trends and developments that are reshaping the way organizations approach quality management.

1. Digital Transformation and Industry 4.0 (Quality 4.0):

Innovation: Industry 4.0, also known as the Fourth Industrial Revolution, is revolutionizing quality management through digital technologies, data analytics, and automation. Quality 4.0 leverages IoT (Internet of Things), AI (Artificial Intelligence), Big Data, and cloud computing to enhance quality monitoring, predictive maintenance, and real-time decision-making.

Impact: Organizations are transitioning from manual data collection and analysis to real-time monitoring and predictive quality control. This enables early defect detection, reduced downtime, and improved overall product and service quality.

Lesson Learned: Embracing digital transformation is not optional but essential for competitiveness and quality excellence. Organizations must invest in technology and data-driven capabilities to stay relevant.

2. Risk-Based Quality Management:

Innovation: The shift towards risk-based quality management acknowledges that not all processes or products pose the same level of risk. Organizations are now prioritizing resources based on risk assessments, focusing efforts where they matter most.

Impact: This approach allows organizations to allocate resources efficiently, focusing on critical areas while streamlining less risky processes. It enhances proactive risk management and quality assurance.

Lesson Learned: Quality management is not a one-size-fits-all endeavor. Tailoring efforts based on risk assessments ensures a more targeted and effective quality strategy.

3. Sustainable Quality Practices:

Innovation: Sustainability and environmental responsibility are becoming integral to quality management. Organizations are adopting sustainable practices that minimize waste, reduce energy consumption, and prioritize ethical sourcing and production.

Impact: Sustainable quality practices not only benefit the planet but also resonate with environmentally-conscious consumers. They enhance brand reputation and contribute to long-term business sustainability.

Lesson Learned: Quality management must evolve to consider the environmental and social impacts of products and processes. Sustainability is not just a trend but a strategic imperative.

4. Quality Systems Integration:

Innovation: Integration of quality management systems with other organizational systems, such as Enterprise Resource Planning (ERP) and Customer Relationship Management (CRM), is streamlining data flow and enhancing overall quality control.

Impact: Improved integration ensures that quality data is readily available to decision-makers across the organization, enabling a more holistic view of quality performance.

Lesson Learned: Siloed quality systems are inefficient. Seamless integration empowers organizations to make informed decisions and enhance overall quality.

5. Continuous Learning and Employee Empowerment:

Innovation: The future of quality management places a strong emphasis on continuous learning and employee empowerment. Organizations are investing in training and development to ensure that employees have the skills and knowledge needed to drive quality improvements.

Impact: Empowered and educated employees are more likely to contribute to innovation and process improvements, leading to enhanced product and service quality.

Lesson Learned: Quality management is not solely the

responsibility of a few experts but a collective effort that involves the entire workforce. Investing in employee development pays dividends in quality.

6. Regulatory Changes and Globalization:

Innovation: The global nature of business requires organizations to navigate an increasingly complex regulatory landscape. Quality management must adapt to comply with evolving international standards and regulations.

Impact: Organizations that stay ahead of regulatory changes are better positioned to ensure compliance, avoid penalties, and maintain product and service quality.

Lesson Learned: Flexibility and agility in adapting to regulatory changes are essential. Organizations must stay informed and be proactive in compliance efforts.

Conclusion:

The future of quality management is marked by innovation, integration, sustainability, and a commitment to excellence.

Organizations that embrace these trends and lessons learned are poised to thrive in a world where quality is not just a standard but a strategic advantage. The path to quality excellence is a continuous journey, and the future promises exciting opportunities for those who embark on it with vision and determination.

Glossary of Terms

Quality management is a field replete with specialized terminology, jargon, and acronyms. To navigate the intricacies of quality management effectively, it's crucial to understand the language used within the discipline. This glossary provides a comprehensive overview of key quality terms and concepts:

1. Quality:

- **Definition:** The degree to which a product or service meets or exceeds customer expectations and fulfills requirements.

- **Significance:** Quality is the ultimate goal of quality management, representing the core principle of delivering value to customers.

2. Total Quality Management (TQM):

- **Definition:** A holistic approach to quality management that focuses on involving all employees in continuous improvement, customer satisfaction, and data-driven decision-making.

- **Significance:** TQM is a comprehensive philosophy that underpins many quality management practices.

3. ISO Standards:

- **Definition:** A series of international standards developed by the International Organization for Standardization (ISO) that define requirements for various aspects of quality management, such as ISO 9001 (Quality Management Systems) and ISO 14001 (Environmental Management Systems).

- **Significance:** ISO standards provide a common framework for quality management practices worldwide.

4. Six Sigma:

- **Definition:** A data-driven methodology aimed at minimizing defects and variations in processes and products to achieve near-perfect quality.

- **Significance:** Six Sigma focuses on reducing variability and improving process capability.

5. Lean Manufacturing:

- **Definition:** A systematic approach to minimizing waste, improving efficiency, and optimizing processes in manufacturing.

- **Significance:** Lean principles, such as Just-In-Time production, are integral to quality improvement.

6. Quality Assurance (QA):

- **Definition:** A proactive process that ensures that products and processes meet specified requirements and standards.

- **Significance:** QA focuses on preventing defects and ensuring compliance.

7. Quality Control (QC):

- **Definition:** A reactive process involving inspections, tests, and measurements to detect and correct defects in products or processes.

- **Significance:** QC aims to identify and rectify deviations from quality standards.

8. Statistical Process Control (SPC):

- **Definition:** The use of statistical methods and techniques to monitor and control processes and maintain product quality.

- **Significance:** SPC involves analyzing process data to make informed decisions about process stability and performance.

9. Root Cause Analysis (RCA):

- **Definition:** A structured process of identifying and addressing the underlying causes of problems or defects.

- **Significance:** RCA helps prevent recurring issues by

addressing their fundamental causes.

10. Pareto Analysis:

- **Definition:** A technique that prioritizes problems or causes based on their frequency or impact.

- **Significance:** Pareto Analysis aids in focusing resources on the most critical quality issues.

11. Fishbone Diagram (Ishikawa):

- **Definition:** A visual tool used to identify the possible causes of a problem or defect, organized into categories resembling a fishbone.

- **Significance:** The diagram helps teams brainstorm and analyze potential causes systematically.

12. Key Performance Indicators (KPIs):

- **Definition:** Quantifiable metrics used to measure and evaluate the performance of processes, products, or organizations.

- **Significance:** KPIs provide actionable insights into quality performance.

13. Continuous Improvement:

- **Definition:** An ongoing effort to enhance processes, products, and services incrementally over time.

- **Significance:** Continuous improvement is a fundamental principle of quality management.

14. Customer Focus:

- **Definition:** A core quality principle that emphasizes meeting and exceeding customer expectations.

- **Significance:** Customer satisfaction is a central tenet of quality management.

15. Supplier Quality Management:

- **Definition:** The process of evaluating, monitoring, and improving the quality of products and services provided by suppliers.

- **Significance:** Supplier quality affects the overall quality of an organization's products and services.

16. Risk-Based Quality Management:

- **Definition:** An approach that prioritizes quality efforts based on risk assessments, focusing on critical areas with the highest potential impact.

- **Significance:** Risk-based quality management enhances efficiency and resource allocation.

This glossary offers a foundational understanding of essential quality terms. It serves as a valuable reference for quality professionals, ensuring clear communication and alignment with quality management principles and practices.

Resources and References

As you reach the final pages of this book by Nikhilesh Mishra, consider it not an ending but a stepping stone. The pursuit of knowledge is an unending journey, and the world of information is boundless.

Discover a World Beyond These Pages

We extend a warm invitation to explore a realm of boundless learning and discovery through our dedicated online platform: **www.nikhileshmishra.com**. Here, you will unearth a carefully curated trove of resources and references to empower your quest for wisdom.

Unleash the Potential of Your Mind

- **Digital Libraries:** Immerse yourself in vast digital libraries, granting access to books, research papers, and academic treasures.

- **Interactive Courses:** Engage with interactive courses and lectures from world-renowned institutions, nurturing your thirst for knowledge.

- **Enlightening Talks:** Be captivated by enlightening talks delivered by visionaries and experts from diverse fields.

- **Community Connections:** Connect with a global community of like-minded seekers, engage in meaningful discussions, and share your knowledge journey.

Your Journey Has Just Begun

Your journey as a seeker of knowledge need not end here. Our website awaits your exploration, offering a gateway to an infinite universe of insights and references tailored to ignite your intellectual curiosity.

Acknowledgments

As I stand at this pivotal juncture, reflecting upon the completion of this monumental work, I am overwhelmed with profound gratitude for the exceptional individuals who have been instrumental in shaping this remarkable journey.

In Loving Memory

To my father, **Late Shri Krishna Gopal Mishra,** whose legacy of wisdom and strength continues to illuminate my path, even in his physical absence, I offer my deepest respect and heartfelt appreciation.

The Pillars of Support

My mother**, Mrs. Vijay Kanti Mishra,** embodies unwavering resilience and grace. Your steadfast support and unwavering faith in my pursuits have been the bedrock of my journey.

To my beloved wife, **Mrs. Anshika Mishra,** your unshakable belief in my abilities has been an eternal wellspring of motivation. Your constant encouragement has propelled me to reach new heights.

My daughter, **Miss Aarvi Mishra,** infuses my life with boundless joy and unbridled inspiration. Your insatiable curiosity serves as a constant reminder of the limitless power of exploration and discovery.

Brothers in Arms

To my younger brothers, **Mr. Ashutosh Mishra** and **Mr. Devashish Mishra,** who have steadfastly stood by my side, offering unwavering support and shared experiences that underscore the strength of familial bonds.

A Journey Shared

This book is a testament to the countless hours of dedication and effort that have gone into its creation. I am immensely grateful for the privilege of sharing my knowledge and insights with a global audience.

Readers, My Companions

To all the readers who embark on this intellectual journey alongside me, your curiosity and unquenchable thirst for knowledge inspire me to continually push the boundaries of understanding in the realm of cloud computing.

With profound appreciation and sincere gratitude,

Nikhilesh Mishra

September 08, 2023

About the Author

Nikhilesh Mishra is an extraordinary visionary, propelled by an insatiable curiosity and an unyielding passion for innovation. With a relentless commitment to exploring the boundaries of knowledge and technology, Nikhilesh has embarked on an exceptional journey to unravel the intricate complexities of our world.

Hailing from the vibrant and diverse landscape of India, Nikhilesh's pursuit of knowledge has driven him to plunge deep into the world of discovery and understanding from a remarkably young age. His unwavering determination and quest for innovation have not only cemented his position as a thought leader but have also earned him global recognition in the ever-evolving realm of technology and human understanding.

Over the years, Nikhilesh has not only mastered the art of translating complex concepts into accessible insights but has also crafted a unique talent for inspiring others to explore the limitless possibilities of human potential.

Nikhilesh's journey transcends the mere boundaries of expertise; it is a transformative odyssey that challenges conventional wisdom and redefines the essence of exploration. His commitment to pushing the boundaries and reimagining the norm serves as a luminous beacon of inspiration to all those who aspire to make a profound impact in the world of knowledge.

As you navigate the intricate corridors of human understanding and innovation, you will not only gain insight into Nikhilesh's expertise but also experience his unwavering dedication to empowering readers like you. Prepare to be enthralled as he seamlessly melds intricate insights with real-world applications, igniting the flames of curiosity and innovation within each reader.

Nikhilesh Mishra's work extends beyond the realm of authorship; it is a reflection of his steadfast commitment to shaping the future of knowledge and exploration. It is an embodiment of his boundless dedication to disseminating wisdom for the betterment of individuals worldwide.

Prepare to be inspired, enlightened, and empowered as you embark on this transformative journey alongside Nikhilesh Mishra. Your understanding of the world will be forever enriched, and your passion for exploration and innovation will reach new heights under his expert guidance.

Sincerely, **A Fellow Explorer**

Notes

Notes

Notes

Notes

Notes

Notes

Notes

Notes

www.ingramcontent.com/pod-product-compliance
Lightning Source LLC
Chambersburg PA
CBHW070917260726
48661CB00003B/740